Early Teaching and Assessment Guide

Sue Bodman and Glen Franklin

University Printing House, Cambridge CB2 8BS, United Kingdom

One Liberty Plaza, 20th Floor, New York, NY 10006, USA

477 Williamstown Road, Port Melbourne, VIC 3207, Australia

314–321, 3rd Floor, Plot 3, Splendor Forum, Jasola District Centre, New Delhi – 110025, India

79 Anson Road, #06–04/06, Singapore 079906

Cambridge University Press is part of the University of Cambridge.

It furthers the University's mission by disseminating knowledge in the pursuit of
education, learning and research at the highest international levels of excellence.

Information on this title: www.cambridge.org/9781108585101

First published 2019

20 19 18 17 16 15 14 13 12 11 10 9 8 7 6 5 4 3 2 1

Printed in Great Britain by CPI Group (UK) Ltd, Croydon CR0 4YY

A catalogue record for this publication is available from the British Library

ISBN 978-1-108-58510-1
Early Teaching and Assessment Guide with Cambridge Elevate

....

....

Contents

Introducing *Cambridge Reading Adventures*

Cambridge Reading Adventures is one of the first Primary reading schemes designed for use by children from all international contexts. To achieve this aim, it moves away from the western-centric approach adopted by many English medium reading schemes. To ensure high quality texts and engaging stories, we went to the very best authors and illustrators from around the world. They have provided an outstanding range and variety of stories and non-fiction, firmly underpinned by a highly successful pedagogy. This pedagogy has been applied by Series Editors Sue Bodman and Glen Franklin of the UCL Institute of Education, ensuring that every page of every book is designed to support the process of learning to read. The series is accompanied by thorough guidance to the teacher, so that every teaching interaction can be planned to develop reading and thinking skills.

Cambridge Reading Adventures provides the young learner with a range of stories, all of which have the kinds of settings, plots and characters which a child growing up anywhere in the world can relate to. This includes a series of stories set in an international school in which the young reader is introduced to the characters Omar, Zara, Hamidi, Beno, Tefo and Leila. Just like the scheme's young readers, Omar and company encounter issues all children will be familiar with such as friendship and disagreement, success and disappointment and even the perils of getting to school. Many stories in the scheme have a contemporary setting designed to reflect life around the world in the 21st Century that the children will recognise, whether at home, in the village or city, or at the supermarket, shopping mall or the beach.

But sometimes the setting is less familiar – with stories about being stranded in a sandstorm or lost at sea.

The scheme also draws on the rich seams of traditional stories from all around the world. The cunning Indonesian mouse deer, Sang Kancil, appears twice, while the legendary Arabic sailor Sinbad also features in two stories. There are traditional tales from China, Africa and other parts of the world.

These are supported at the younger end with a range of humorous stories based around animal characters, like 'Leopard and his Spots' and 'The Hot Day'.

A further rich vein of stories arises in the later book bands with stories based on actual historical settings, such as 'Mei and the Pirate Queen' and 'The Silk Road'.

The use of highly relevant settings and humorous and exciting contexts ensures the teacher can find material that children want to read.

An equally high quality range of non-fiction titles provides balance and breadth to the series. Starting at the very earliest bands, and including information books, reports, recounts and instructional texts, non-fiction titles cover a range of topics of great relevance to the wider curriculum, with full links provided to international curricula in the back of each book. Texts are designed to give the young reader the opportunity to learn the key skills for navigating non-fiction books, and properly utilising features like tables, maps, fact boxes, captions, indexes and glossaries. Teachers are provided with quality materials to teach these skills.

Great care has been taken to choose topics which are directly relevant to the young child growing up in the 21st Century, such as computers, shopping malls, journeying by train and plane and even mobile phone technology. In addition, there is a rich strand of books about the natural world – as it was (such as 'Pterosaur!' and 'Animals of the Ice Age') and as it is now ('All Kinds of Plants', 'Earthquakes' and 'The Great Migration').

For the teacher, *Cambridge Reading Adventures* offers a thorough and dependable teaching structure and comprehensive guidance for teaching guided reading. For a young child learning to read, whether in Bangkok, Dubai, London, Mumbai or Bogota, *Cambridge Reading Adventures* promises a rich, fully supportive and fascinating journey towards becoming an independent reader.

The UCL Institute of Education's International Literacy Centre (ILC) promotes quality and efficacy in literacy education from age 3 to 13 (Early Years Foundation Stage to Key Stage 3). Over the last 25 years, the ILC, formally the European Centre for Reading Recovery, has successfully trained many thousands of teachers, including those from international contexts, to provide effective literacy teaching through a range of interventions and classroom approaches.

As well as providing high-quality professional support for teachers and teacher educators, the ILC develops materials and professional development opportunities to support teachers to teach literacy skills effectively. One of these is Book Banding, the definitive system for organising texts for guided reading to support early Primary reading, which is currently used in most UK Primary schools. Most recently, Book Banding principles and official listings were published in *Which Book and Why? Using Book Bands and book levels for guided reading in Key Stage 1* (Bodman and Franklin, 2014).

Sue Bodman and Glen Franklin, the Series Editors of *Cambridge Reading Adventures*, are National Leaders at the International Literacy Centre

Introduction

Overview of the Teaching and Assessment Guide

The *Cambridge Reading Adventures Teaching and Assessment Guide* is designed to support teachers to deliver effective guided reading lessons, and to make meaningful assessments that serve to ensure children achieve success.

The *Teaching and Assessment Guide* is divided into three sections:

Section One: Teaching Reading

This section explores the nature of reading. Based on the underlying principle that reading is a meaningful activity carried out for purpose and pleasure, the range of reading in classrooms is explored and the different features of fiction and non-fiction reading are considered. The nature of guided reading as a specific teaching method is explained. The philosophy and practice of book-banding for guided reading is outlined, with clear examples provided.

This section is predominantly to inform teachers, and provides the theoretical background to the teaching approach employed in *Cambridge Reading Adventures*.

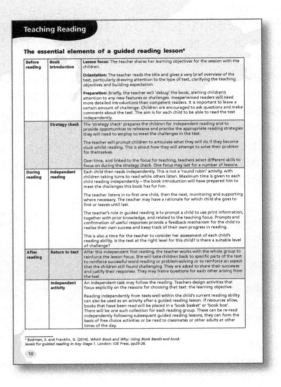

Section Two: Book By Book Overview

Each individual text in *Cambridge Reading Adventures* is explained in detail, helping teachers to select the right book for the right group of children. Teaching guidance is provided for the fiction and non-fiction texts at each band.

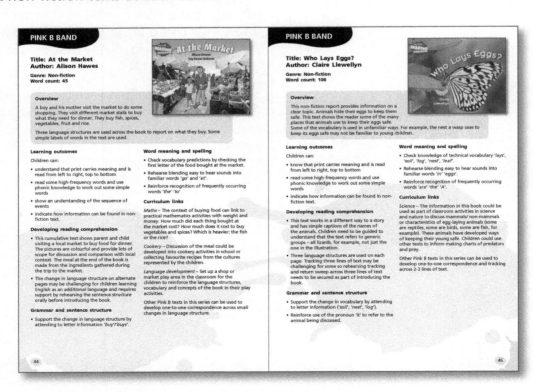

Section Three: Assessment for guided reading

This section offers teachers a benchmark text at each band to support teacher decision-making in assessing whether the child is ready to move to the next band in *Cambridge Reading Adventures*.

A range of support materials is provided for assessing children's reading comprehension. Guidance on how to take, record and analyse running records of text reading is provided. The overall observations are then pulled together as a comprehensive and informative summary of the child's reading behaviour at that band.

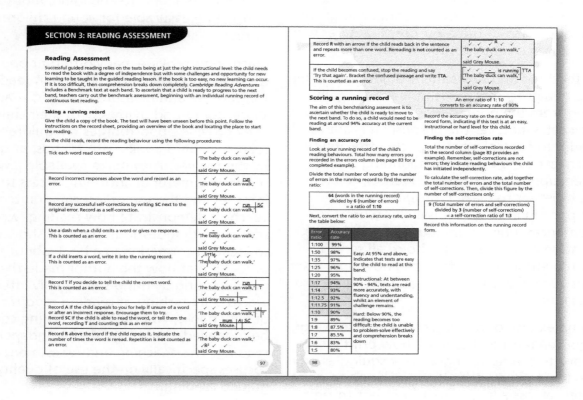

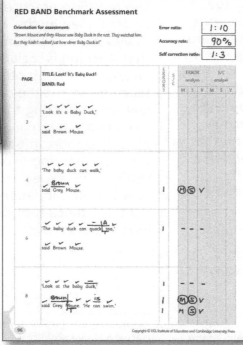

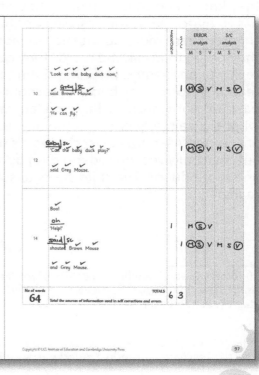

SECTION 1: TEACHING READING

What is Reading?

When you pick up a book, open a web-link or read a set of instructions, what is it that directs what you are doing? You will have had a purpose in mind that shapes how you read and what you do – you might want to settle down and read your new novel, or to check what time your flight is, or you might need to set up your new tablet computer. Sometimes reading will be for pleasure, sometimes for work or to glean information; each of these purposes requires you to read, but in a subtly different way.

In this Teaching and Assessment Guide, we define reading as a process by which the reader gains meaning from the printed word[1]. Reading is a complex act, whatever the purpose: it requires the reader to control many aspects – the ability to match letters to their corresponding sound (grapheme/phoneme correspondence); to blend sounds together to make words; to look for known parts in longer, multisyllabic words; to read sentences, understanding how word order, punctuation and vocabulary choice all serve to convey the author's intention; to know how texts are constructed and to understand their purpose and meaning.

This complex task of reading starts with looking[2]. Beginner readers need to learn how print works. They have to attend to those black squiggles on a white page, to know that they track one-to-one accurately across a line of text from left-to-right in English, to begin to notice letters and words they know, and to understand that what they say has to match what they can see on the page. As children learn more about the alphabetic code, they begin to break the words they can see into separate phonemes, blending them together to read the word. They begin to recognise recurring parts of words such as 'ing' and 'ed' and they link what they already know to the new words they encounter. As more and more words become automatically recognised, reading becomes faster and more fluent. The child starts to sound like a reader.

Young readers seek to make meaning from their very earliest encounters with print. Often the very first word they read is their name. Books for beginner readers provide strong language structures and make good use of illustrations to support meaning. Vocabulary matches the child's oral language. Fiction books have a strong sense of story. Non-fiction books have genuine information to convey. Most importantly, books for young readers are engaging, motivating and above all pleasurable for young children learning to read.

Classrooms provide many different opportunities for the young reader to engage in reading for purpose and pleasure. Teachers read and share stories and rhymes with their children. They provide opportunities for children to read and share books with friends, or quietly by themselves. They make available a wealth of reading material, including access to the Internet and the use of information technology. Teachers demonstrate how reading 'works' in shared reading sessions; perhaps showing how to locate information in a book about animals, or looking at how the author made the story more exciting by using some really interesting words. All teaching of reading requires good quality books, whether the teaching context be modelled, shared, guided or independent reading. This Teaching and Assessment Guide focuses specifically on the use of quality texts in guided reading.

Guided reading operates alongside shared and independent reading in the classroom. The teaching practice of guided reading is underpinned by the work of theorists such as Vygotsky and Bruner. These theories hold that learning is socially constructed through engagement with others. Teachers target their teaching at just the right point in their children's learning, enabling them to do something they would have been unable to do alone. Teachers provide opportunities for children to rehearse this new learning in a supportive, collaborative setting, and expect the children to take on this new learning independently: 'what a child can do with assistance today she will be able to do by herself tomorrow'[3].

---

[1] Bodman, S. and Franklin, G. (2014). *Which Book and Why: Using Book Bands and book levels for guided reading in Key Stage 1*. London: IOE Press

---

[2] Clay, M. M. (2005). *Literacy Lessons Designed for Individuals – Part 2: Teaching Procedures*. Auckland, N.Z.: Heinemann

[3] Vygotsky, L.S. (1978). *Mind in Society*. Cambridge, MA: Harvard University Press

What is Guided Reading?

Guided reading is a teaching methodology; a way of organising teaching and assessment. It has specific goals. The teacher aims to support the children in reading text for themselves, putting into practice all the aspects of word and letter learning and reading strategies that have been taught previously. To do this, the teacher organises the class into small groups. Each group is carefully matched to a band through assessment. The teacher has a specific learning objective for the group and carefully choses a different book for each; one that helps her guide the learning and thinking of the children in that group. The book offers some challenge to the young readers and, by using awareness of the children's knowledge and experience, careful preparation of the text and the process of literacy acquisition, the teacher offers the right level of support to enable all the children to read the text independently. Active participation at each child's own level of attainment is the aim of guided reading.

A guided reading lesson has some key features:

- Small groups, usually between 4 to 8

- Similar level of attainment in the group

- A copy of the text for each child and the teacher

- A new text in each guided reading lesson

- Reading strategies are applied, reinforced and extended

- The text can be accessed easily (at or above 90% accuracy)

- The children read independently whilst the teacher works with each individual child in turn (as opposed to reading aloud around the group)

- Teacher interactions focus on prompts and praise to support

- From the earliest colour bands, each child is required to think about problem-solving strategies

- It follows a guided learning structure, as follows.

The Guided Reading Teaching Sequence

The guided reading teaching sequence creates:

- an opportunity for the teacher to teach reading strategies explicitly at a text level appropriate to each child.

- an effective and efficient way to provide instruction within a structure which enables the teacher to respond to the range of ability in a class.

- the opportunity for independent reading practice on the right levels of text for each child.

- a context to use and reinforce letters, words and strategies being taught as part of a classroom reading programme, resulting in systematic teaching.

- a focus on reading comprehension.

The table on page 10 gives an overview of the generic teaching sequence for guided reading. All guided reading lessons follow this structure, whether the children are well advanced in the process of learning to read or just beginning to learn. The emphasis and content of part of the sequence will be shaped to support the learner, whatever their current competences.

Teaching Reading

The essential elements of a guided reading lesson[4]

Before reading	**Book introduction**	**Lesson focus:** The teacher shares her learning objectives for the session with the children.
		Orientation: The teacher reads the title and gives a very brief overview of the text, particularly drawing attention to the type of text, clarifying the teaching objectives and building expectation.
		Preparation: Briefly, the teacher will 'debug' the book, alerting children's attention to any new features or challenges. Inexperienced readers will need more detailed introductions than competent readers. It is important to leave a certain amount of challenge. Children are encouraged to ask questions and make comments about the text. The aim is for each child to be able to read the text independently.
	Strategy check	The 'strategy check' prepares the children for independent reading and to provide opportunities to rehearse and practise the appropriate reading strategies they will need to employ to meet the challenges in the text.
		The teacher will prompt children to articulate what they will do if they become stuck whilst reading. This is about how they will attempt to solve their problem for themselves.
		Over time, and linked to the focus for teaching, teachers select different skills to focus on during the strategy check. One focus may last for a number of lessons.
During reading	**Independent reading**	Each child then reads independently. This is not a 'round robin' activity, with children taking turns to read while others listen. Maximum time is given to each child reading independently – the book introduction will have prepared him to meet the challenges this book has for him.
		The teacher listens in to first one child, then the next, monitoring and supporting where necessary. The teacher may have a rationale for which child she goes to first or leaves until last.
		The teacher's role in guided reading is to prompt a child to use print information, together with prior knowledge, and related to the teaching focus. Prompts and confirmation of useful responses provide a feedback mechanism for the child to realise their own success and keep track of their own progress in reading.
		This is also a time for the teacher to consider her assessment of each child's reading ability. Is the text at the right level for this child? Is there a suitable level of challenge?
After reading	**Return to text**	After this independent first reading, the teacher works with the whole group to reinforce the lesson focus. She will take children back to specific parts of the text to reinforce successful word reading or problem-solving or to reinforce an aspect that the children still found challenging. They are asked to share their successes and justify their responses. They may frame questions for each other arising from the text.
	Independent activity	An independent task may follow the reading. Teachers design activities that focus explicitly on the reasons for choosing that text: the learning objective.
		Reading independently from texts well within the child's current reading ability can also be used as an activity after a guided reading lesson. If resources allow, books that have been read will be placed in a 'book basket' or 'book box'. There will be one such collection for each reading group. These can be re-read independently following subsequent guided reading lessons, they can form the basis of free choice activities or be read to classmates or other adults at other times of the day.

[4] Bodman, S. and Franklin, G. (2014). *Which Book and Why: Using Book Bands and book levels for guided reading in Key Stage 1*. London: IOE Press, pp25-26.

Guided Reading Record Sheet

Class: Group:

Names:	Date:
....	Text:
....	Band:
....	

Key Learning Goals for the lesson:

Learning Objective and Success Criteria

Planning notes/Key questions/Comments

Child	Notes and observations

11

Reading Fiction Books

Fiction is all about story-telling. As readers, we choose stories that excite, intrigue, puzzle or frighten us. We look for stories that reaffirm our own lives or take us to lives we can only imagine. Haven[5] described stories as 'the primary roadmap for understanding, making sense of, remembering and planning our lives'.

What makes a story? It has been said that there are just a small number of basic story themes, and these have been around since humans first began to tell stories: monsters and villains are overcome; the poor become rich through good fortune or wrong-doing; quests are made to seek to do something or to right a wrong; voyages to unknown worlds are undertaken and the adventurer returns to tell the tale. Stories can be funny or tragic, or a mixture of both.

Sinbad and the Giant Roc, Turquoise band

Fiction writers rework or revise these themes to continue to tell new stories. They intermingle the themes – a quest may have elements of comedy; a monster story might have a rags-to-riches ending. Writers take those basic plots and situations and, by reinventing them, they make it their own.

Yu and the Giant Flood, Gold band

Young children encounter fiction from the earliest age. Long before they can talk, babies and toddlers listen to stories read to them. They demand to hear their favourite books over and over again. From these experiences, they begin to gain a sense of story, implicitly picking up on those story themes. Through hearing stories, they discover how stories work – even the simplest stories employ a structure that moves from a clear beginning to a resolved end. They learn that there are good characters and bad, and begin to empathise with those who are lost or need help. They discover magical lands and faraway places, and look at their everyday world through the eyes of the story teller. The literature-rich school classroom builds upon the story experiences children bring with them from home when they start school.

Jamila Finds a Friend, Pink A band

When writing a book, an author always has the potential reader in mind. A book written to be shared by a parent or carer with a young child sitting on her lap will be a very different sort of book to that which an older reader would chose to read on their own in bed at night. The writer's purpose and audience dictates the style, scope, vocabulary and even the length of the text. The fiction books in *Cambridge Reading Adventures* have been written specifically to be used in a small group guided reading context, led by a teacher, to support the teaching of reading.

---

[5] Page 3, Haven, K. (2007). *Story Proof: The Science Behind the Startling Power of Story.* Westport, CT: Libraries Unlimited.

Reading is, first and foremost, about making meaning. Books for guided reading are designed to support the development of comprehension from the very beginning. The earliest books are short. They have simple language structures that mirror the natural pattern of spoken English. They are illustrated clearly to match the written message, the subject matter is appropriate to children's experiences, and care is taken to choose words and phrases that are within the young reader's own conceptual understanding. Words are phonically decodable or high-frequency, with nouns and verbs supported strongly by the grammar and meaning.

Sang Kancil and the Tiger, Turquoise band

Omar can Help, Red band

The teaching notes at the back of each book offer guidance to teachers for teaching inference-making in story. Many of the follow-up suggestions provide activities designed to support developing comprehension. This Teaching and Assessment Guide describes each story in detail, and explains the teaching opportunities featured in each individual text as children progress through the banded gradient of challenge (see page 28).

As reading progresses, stories require more inferential links to be made. Inference is crucial to reading comprehension. Readers have to move beyond the literal meaning of the actual words on the page, to read 'between the lines' to fully comprehend the author's intention. Kintsch and Rawson[6] describe this as the reader forming a mental or 'situation' model of the story. Readers, they argue, use their prior knowledge, their understanding of the subject and of how stories work, to fill in the gaps. Fiction books in *Cambridge Reading Adventures* have strong story structures to support comprehension. Themes build upon children's own experiences by placing new characters in familiar events, or through traditional retellings of tales from around the world. As books become longer, stories are often sustained over two or more events, or over time. Language structures become more complex, with the meaning sometimes implied by the word order or the author's choice of vocabulary.

[6] Kintsch, W., & Rawson, K. A. (2005). Comprehension. In M. J. Snowling & C. Hulme (Eds.), *The Science of Reading: A Handbook* (pp. 209-226). Malden, MA: Blackwell.

Reading Non-fiction Books

If we stopped and thought about the reading we have done over the last 24 hours, a large proportion of that reading is likely to have been non-fiction: consulting a recipe book to check the amount of sugar needed; following a set of instructions to load a new computer programme; searching the Internet for the best deals on flights to our chosen holiday location. Non-fiction reading forms an integral part of our daily lives.

Efficient readers modify the way they read according the nature of the text[7]. They will have a purpose when reading it - to answer a question or to find out more information. Reading non-fiction for a purpose is crucial – the reader has to be able to ask 'what do I want to get from this book, and why?'. That is not meant to imply that non-fiction is not pleasurable. A young child who loves dinosaurs will be motivated to read a book about prehistoric animals simply because of that interest. Likewise, reading a good story can lead the reader to want explore the real-life setting or events that provided the stimulus for the plot. However, there are clear differences between story books and books predominantly written for information, and they need to be taught differently.

Pterosaur!, Purple band

Whilst not a definitive list, it is generally agreed that there are six main non-fiction purposes or 'genre' types[8]:

- to recount or retell an event

- to report or describe something

- to instruct or to describe a procedure

- to explain how things work or how they came to be

- to discuss a particular issue, acknowledging different points of view

- to persuade the reader towards a particular position upheld by the writer.

Non-fiction authors, when writing for an experienced audience, rarely delineate so clearly: a book about a farm, for example, might include elements of instruction on how to care for animals mixed with aspects of persuasion about the benefits of organic farming. Non-fiction books written specifically for young children learning to read will present one type of genre very clearly, following the structural organisation and language features that support that purpose for reading. (See the table on page 15.)

Our Senses, Red band

Early non-fiction texts in *Cambridge Reading Adventures* focus predominantly on recounts, reports and instructions. Children's own personal experiences and familiar settings support their comprehension. As reading progresses, texts in the scheme begin to include the other more complex genres, and will move into subject matter less familiar to the reader. Non-fiction features, such as glossaries, indexes, facts boxes, maps and diagrams are gradually introduced throughout, beginning with labels and captions. As each new feature is introduced, teachers need to demonstrate how these are used to support reading for meaning and purpose.

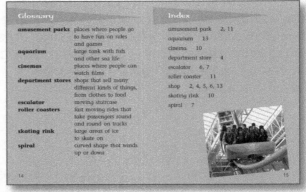

Super Malls, Orange band

---

[7] Wray, D. and Lewis, M. (1997). *Extending Literacy: Children Reading and Writing Non-fiction.* London, UK: Routledge.

[8] Bodman, S. and Franklin, G. (2014). *Which Book and Why Using Book Bands and Book Levels for Guided Reading in Key Stage 1.* London: IOE Press.

Purpose	Structural organisation	Language features
Recount	• A sequence of events written in chronological order	• Written in the first (I/we) or third (he/she/they) person • Past tense verbs to indicate the event being retold has already occurred • The sequence of events is indicated by temporal connectives (first, next, later).
Report	• Commonly non-chronological: the sequence is determined by the component parts.	• Written in the present tense • Addresses the subject generically – not about specific things or people.
Instruction	• Chronologically sequenced steps, sometimes numbered. • May include diagrams	• Uses imperative verbs • Addresses the general reader • May include language of sequence (first, then, after that)
Explanation	• Steps organised in a logical sequence to explain or describe the process • Often use diagrams and cycles	• Written in the present tense • Temporal and causal connectives (because, in order to) used
Discussion	• Presents differing points of view • Draws a conclusion based on the argument presented.	• Written in the present tense • Connectives link the points being made (however, therefore). • Addresses the reader more generally
Persuasion	• Clear statement of the concern to be addressed • Logically sequence leading to a conclusion	• Written in the present tense • Use of powerful, often emotive language to put over the point of view

When using *Cambridge Reading Adventures* non-fiction books in guided reading, teachers select books according to the purpose for reading. They make links with the children's personal experiences and with the classroom curriculum. Good book choice is crucial to support the particular non-fiction reading skill teachers want to teach during the guided reading lesson. The teaching notes at the back of each book offer support for teaching non-fiction reading effectively. Guidance is provided to help teachers decide on the appropriate book choice to meet the needs of their group. Many of the follow-up suggestions provide activities designed to develop non-fiction reading skills.

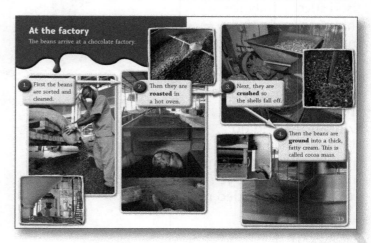

How Chocolate is Made, Turquoise band

Introduction to Book Banding

Effective teaching in guided reading needs to offer materials with the right amount of challenge. That doesn't mean finding books with the same letters, words or sentences in, but books that allow the young reader to use what he knows to solve problems encountered in a text. He does this by using the letters and words he does know as anchors to keep hold of the meaning, whilst working out the unknown letters and words for himself. 'Bands' of books are 'collections' or 'groups' of books. Each band shares the text characteristics (for example, phonic complexity of words, grammatical challenges, layout of text on the page, role of the illustrations) and offers the same level of challenge. The stories, the types of text and the sentence structures within each book are very different. Banding offers support for both the teacher and the child, offering consistency of expectation but a range of language and meaning contexts in which to reinforce active reading and problem-solving. It is a way of analysing the amount of challenge in books for guided reading.

Book Banding is also a way of organising books for guided reading. Each band is given a colour and has a clear set of learning and teaching objectives associated with it. Teachers can organise their book collections for guided reading by colour and use that system to monitor and assess progression in reading. Banding has been used successfully for this purpose in the majority of schools in the UK. *Cambridge Reading Adventures* has been banded using the UCL Institute of Education banding system[9], which bands all of the guided reading materials currently in print. This means you can integrate *Cambridge Reading Adventures* into your existing banded resources.

Using bands to group children

Colour bands allow the teacher to be guided by the needs of the child when choosing a book. First, you identify the band at which the child can read with a rate of accuracy between 90 and 94%. Then, you look closely at the assessment record of the child's reading to determine the skills and knowledge that the child needs to learn next. (The section on how to assess reading is on page 78). Then, you choose a text that presents opportunities for learning that link back to the child's needs identified through assessment. By finding the instructional level for each individual child, you can gather together a small group of children working at the same band and work with them in a guided reading context.

Using bands to extend reading mileage

When you know which book band the groups of children in your class are working at, you will be able to select books at the same band with confidence, knowing that they are the right level for each group. Having the choice of lots of books within the child's reading competence will mean that you now choose books for children to read for pleasure in independent reading times. You can do this by selecting stories and texts that are the band below the one you are using for guided reading lessons. For example, children reading at Blue band in guided reading will be able to access Yellow band texts with ease; they will be ideal for independent reading and free choice reading activities.

Selection of Pink A books

---

[9] Bodman, S. and Franklin, G. (2014). *Which Book and Why: Using Book Bands and book levels for guided reading in Key Stage 1*. London: IOE Press

Using bands to support children learning in an additional language

Learning to read in an additional language presents particular challenges. *Cambridge Reading Adventures* supports second language learning in a number of ways:

- Texts provide a good model of English to support the second language learner to hear, practise, and then predict and use in their own reading and writing

- Challenges are carefully phased in order to ensure success and comprehension throughout all reading lessons

- Vocabulary is supported by clear illustrations in both fiction and non-fiction texts

- Introduction of words that need to be decoded is carefully considered to ensure progression in word reading skills

- Links to the wider curriculum are made so that vocabulary and language structures encountered in reading can be reinforced in other subject study

- Guidance for the teacher ensures that language and reading comprehension are at the heart of every guided reading lesson.

Banding Progression

Band	Colour
1A	Pink A
1B	Pink B
2	Red
3	Yellow
4	Blue
5	Green
6	Orange
7	Turquoise
8	Purple
9	Gold
10	White

Bands are arranged into colour groups that support the reader for the very earliest stages of learning to read (Pink band A and B) to becoming an independent reader (White band and beyond).

Bands 1 to 4 are presented here in the Early Teaching and Assessment Guide.

The features and characteristics of texts at each band are described in the next section.

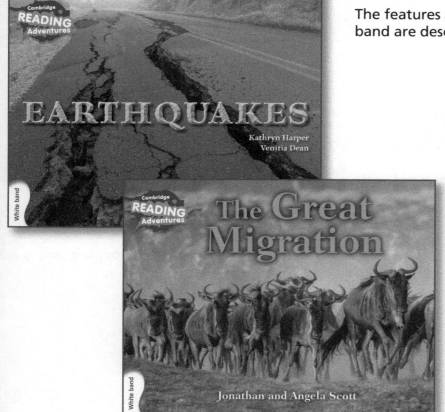

A selection of White band books

Pink A

Pink A texts are designed for children just beginning to read, allowing them to behave like a reader by moving across the text from left to right, return to the left hand side for a new line and to match the spoken word to the print. Fully punctuated throughout, the texts are between 20 and 60 words in length. One repeated sentence structure that is heavily supported by picture information gives plenty of opportunities for children to experience early reading success.

Fiction

Familiar situations and settings provide the context for Pink A stories, maximising opportunities for developing vocabulary.

Simple stories use natural language patterns.

Text placed consistently on each page of the book.

Mum puts apples
in the trolley.

Arif goes Shopping: pages 2-3

A small number of high frequency words are used across Pink A so that the reader can become very familiar with the most useful words in written language.

Clear information in the illustrations supports the reader to use known letters and begin to use them actively in reading.

Non-fiction

Topics are familiar to the children - needing a home, the food we eat, wanting to play, for example. Texts provide opportunities to develop book-handling skills, learning how to focus on print and meeting a range of high frequency words. Sentence structures are kept short and simple. All of the non-fiction texts at Pink A are simple, non-chronological reports of observable facts.

Page layout is uncluttered allowing a focus on directional and one-to-one correspondence skills.

The one change is in a highly prominent place in the sentence.

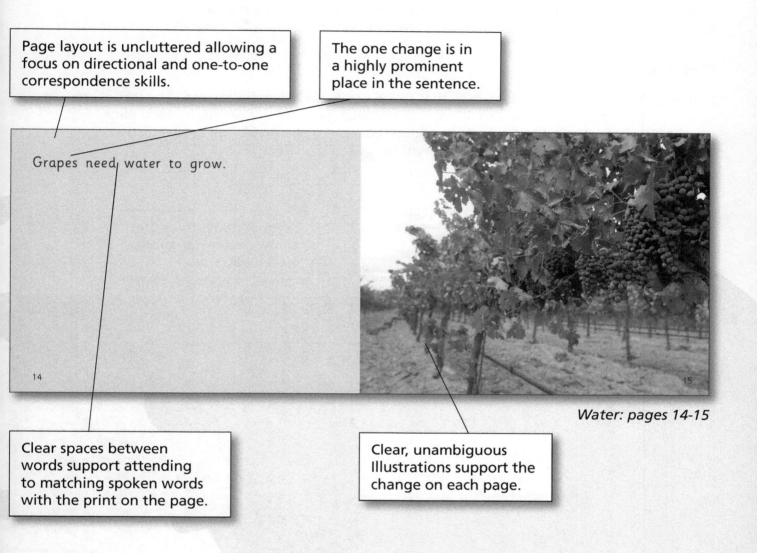

Grapes need water to grow.

14

15

Water: pages 14-15

Clear spaces between words support attending to matching spoken words with the print on the page.

Clear, unambiguous Illustrations support the change on each page.

PINK B Book Band Reading Characteristics

Pink B

Pink B offers repetitive texts using slightly longer language structures. Texts between 35 and 100 words in length may have two or three sentence structures. This consolidates and extends one-to-one correspondence skills. Several sentences on each page reinforces return sweep.

Whilst support via clear illustrations is continued, now attention to word and letter information is required to check oral predictions. Careful word choice results in many opportunities to look across a word from left to right to begin early decoding skills. Exclamation marks and question marks are used to develop reading for meaning.

Fiction

Fiction at Pink B uses natural language that follows children's speech patterns. The stories are simple, involving repeated events with one or two changes, often of nouns, on each page. Familiar settings are used to support the young reader to make oral language predictions that can be monitored against print information.

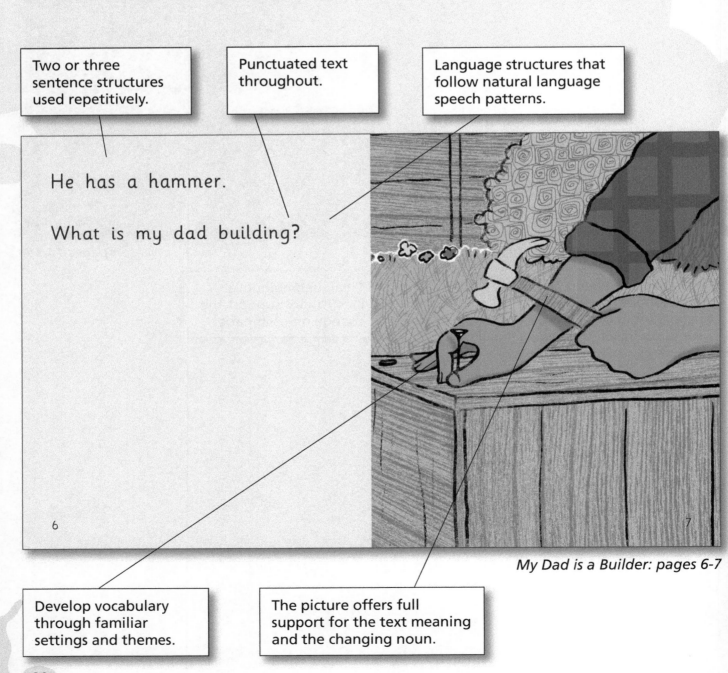

Two or three sentence structures used repetitively.

Punctuated text throughout.

Language structures that follow natural language speech patterns.

He has a hammer.

What is my dad building?

My Dad is a Builder: pages 6-7

Develop vocabulary through familiar settings and themes.

The picture offers full support for the text meaning and the changing noun.

Non-fiction

Topics in the non-fiction range at Pink B are clearly focused – what needs water, how to look after animals, where do animals lay their eggs, for example. The reports are simple and direct. Language structures are used repetitively. Attention needs to be given to print detail as sentences are longer and a greater range of words are used. Language is natural, though does include some reporting structures when they are simple and short; *Animals need …. ,* for example.

Two or three changes on most pages.

Many opportunities to consolidate a small number of high frequency words.

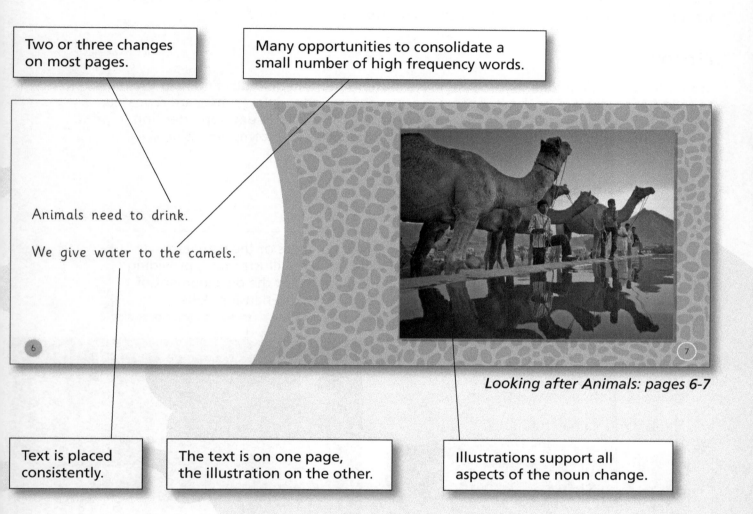

Animals need to drink.

We give water to the camels.

Looking after Animals: pages 6-7

Text is placed consistently.

The text is on one page, the illustration on the other.

Illustrations support all aspects of the noun change.

Red

Texts have story elements that lend themselves to developing retelling and sequencing skills. Now sentence structures are less repetitive. This means that the reader has to pay more consistent attention to letter and word information and rely less on oral prediction. Helping the child to look more consciously is supported by providing slight changes in the order of words within repeated structures. Now that directional skills are secure, there is more variation in page design and presentation of the text.

The texts are slightly longer than at Pink, and children can begin to extend their high frequency word knowledge. Text length ranges from 55 to 135 words.

Fiction

Stories have one clear idea on each page. Illustrations support that idea and help the reader to follow the sequence of the story. Sentences are short and simple. Phrases are repeated, often with small changes that are designed to support the child to develop attention to print. Illustrations provide full support for the development of reading comprehension skills.

The main ideas of the story are offered in the illustrations, providing full support for the development of reading comprehension skills.

Repeated sentence patterns include high frequency words.

Goat will not go to bed.
'Come on, Goat,' says Dev.
'Here is an apple for you.'

8

9

Bedtime on the Farm: pages 8-9

Sentences are short, clear and straightforward and follow children's speech patterns.

Opportunities to decode simple, regular words that are repeated throughout the text.

Non-fiction

Directional skills are now established so Red band books can begin to introduce non-fiction features. Simple labelled diagrams and contents pages are also used at Red band. The same range of high frequency words is used in non-fiction texts so that reading vocabulary is being built in non-fiction experiences too. Topics extend the children's understanding of the world they live in – the weather, creatures in the sea, how we perceive the world around us and the homes we live in. Text is displayed on left hand and right hand pages, occasionally using speech bubbles to provide further commentary.

Clear support for the text through illustrations.

More variation in position of print on the page.

Smelling

Here is my nose.

I smell with my nose.

8

I can smell the flower.

9

Our Senses: pages 8-9

Non-fiction texts use photographs but also drawings when appropriate.

Texts provide opportunities to read simple words by sounding out and blending phonemes left to right.

Yellow

Yellow band books create the context to develop use of sentence structure in reading. Texts utilise longer sentences, a greater range of sentence structures and a wider range of vocabulary to extend reading skills. Longer sentences are supported by shorter sentences so that the increase in challenge is measured and supportive. Repeated words and phrases are now used to create emphasis and tension in the stories, rather than as a device to enable the teacher to focus on building high frequency vocabulary knowledge.

Fiction

Clearly structured stories relating to easy-to-understand concepts provide a context to ask children to relate one text to another. Punctuation supports the child to read with phrasing and expression. Characters in Yellow band texts have become more developed and word choice supports a fuller interpretation of feelings and motivation.

Familiar phonemes can be blended to check oral predictions of context words.

Punctuation supports the use of grammar and oral language rhythms.

Stories may involve imaginary happenings within the framework of familiar experiences

Snail met a spider.
'Do you live here?' he said.
'Yes, I live in a web,' said Spider.

'Can I live here, too?' said Snail.
'No,' said Spider. 'You're too heavy.'

A House for Snail: pages 8-9

Familiar spoken language structures support the development of phrased reading.

A range of simple contractions are used as part of natural language structures.

Non-fiction

Non-fiction texts have a range of text layouts and devices to support meaning whilst illustrations begin to offer less direct support since the word reading skills of the young reader facilitate accurate decoding of simple phonically regular words. Non-fiction texts are laid out in different ways, and expand the range of non-fiction features to labelled diagrams and index sections.

Text remains well spaced so that directional and matching skills can be rehearsed on clear text layout.

Illustrations, both photographs and drawings, offer clear support for the text, but the reader needs to pay close attention to print.

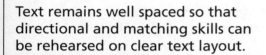

In the Classroom
The first lesson is Maths.
We learn about numbers.

The next lesson is English.
The teacher reads a story.
We sit and listen.

6

7

My School: pages 6-7

Pages have several opportunities to undertake a return sweep.

Texts have between 3 and 5 lines on each page.

Blue

Word complexity increases at Blue band. A growing number of high frequency words appear in both predictable and unusual positions in a language structure, reinforcing word recognition of the most frequently used words in English. Simple two-syllable words are used at Blue. These are well supported by illustrations and give good opportunities to build segmenting and syllabification skills within a supportive context for the learner.

Words feature orthographic patterns that have alternative pronunciations. This calls for an integration of phonic knowledge and language skills.

The few repeated language and phrase patterns are now much longer and are used as refrains. Illustrations are supportive, but do not present the text contents precisely with some inferences needing to be made.

Number of lines on each page can be between 2 and 6, requiring flexible use of return sweep skills across long and short lines of text. Word counts range between 180 and 320.

Fiction

Stories follow the structure of simple fables and tales, often using personalised animal characters to provide texts which develop simple characters to empathise with. Stories often have several characters. Literary language is integrated with natural language patterns and direct speech.

| Longer sentences alongside natural language | Identify constituent parts of unfamiliar two-syllable words to read correctly. | Attending to punctuation is vital to gaining the full meaning and reading with expression |

'Hello,' said the cricket.
'Can I help you, little ant?'

A big tear rolled down the ant's face.

8

'I'm lost!' said the ant.
'Please help me find my nest!'

'Jump on my back,' said the cricket.

9

Lost: pages 8-9

| Simple contractions are used in direct speech. | Sentence patterns vary across any one page – independent clauses, imperatives, questions, reported speech, for example. |

Non-fiction

Texts now include a greater range of types of non-fiction genre. Abstract terms and impersonal sentence structures are used, in keeping with non-fiction styles and language use. Choice of vocabulary becomes more topic-specific, with some simple and commonly-used technical terms included.

Language relates to the specific context.

Lines on a page can range from two to six.

Two-syllable words are well supported by the illustration and the meaning.

The train starts to move.
It makes a rumbling noise.
I look out of the window.

'Oh, look,' I say. 'The platform outside is moving!'

'No,' laughs Mum. 'We are moving!'

10

11

My First Train Trip: pages 10-11

Simple synonyms are used in recounts.

Text remains well-spaced with changes in idea supported by a slightly larger space.

Title	Band	Fiction / Non-fiction
Arif Goes Shopping	PINK A	F
Jamila Finds a Friend	PINK A	F
A Hot Day	PINK A	F
Packing my Bag	PINK A	F
Please Stop, Sara!	PINK A	F
Water	PINK A	NF
The Sun is Up	PINK A	NF
Games	PINK A	NF
Animal Homes	PINK A	NF
Photos	PINK A	F
The Tractor	PINK A	F
I Can Help	PINK A	NF
My Dad is a Builder	PINK B	F
The Last Lemon	PINK B	F
Leela Can Skate	PINK B	F
Omar's First Day at School	PINK B	F
Our Den	PINK B	F
Looking After Animals	PINK B	NF
At the Market	PINK B	NF
Who Lays Eggs?	PINK B	NF
Where do they Grow?	PINK B	NF
Hello, Baby	PINK B	F
School Lunch	PINK B	F
Where are you Going?	PINK B	F
Bedtime on the Farm	RED	F
Leopard and his Spots	RED	F
The Enormous Watermelon	RED	F
Omar can Help	RED	F
Seagull	RED	F
Look! It's Baby Duck	RED	F
Our Senses	RED	NF
In the Sea	RED	NF
The Weather Today	RED	NF
Houses and Homes	RED	NF
Imani's Library Book	RED	F
What Little Kitten Wants	RED	F

SECTION 2: BOOK BY BOOK OVERVIEW

Title	Band	Fiction / Non-fiction
A House for Snail	YELLOW	F
Diego Fandango	YELLOW	F
Late for School	YELLOW	F
Oh Bella!	YELLOW	F
Little Tiger Hu Can Roar	YELLOW	F
My School	YELLOW	NF
Playgrounds	YELLOW	NF
Stars	YELLOW	NF
Help!	YELLOW	F
The Boy Who Said No	YELLOW	F
The Big City	YELLOW	NF
Where are my Shoes?	YELLOW	F
Lost!	BLUE	F
Suli's Big Race	BLUE	F
A Day at the Museum	BLUE	F
It's Much Too Early!	BLUE	F
The Pumpkin Monster	BLUE	F
My First Train Trip	BLUE	NF
Making a Car	BLUE	NF
All Kinds of Plants	BLUE	NF
On the Track	BLUE	NF
Crabs	BLUE	NF
The Show and Tell Day	BLUE	F
The Big Pancake	BLUE	F
The Mean Monkey	BLUE	F

Title: Arif Goes Shopping
Author: Charlotte al-Qadi

Genre: Fiction
Word count: 42

Overview

Arif and Mum go shopping. Mum puts her shopping in the trolley. Arif tries to help by picking items or helping Mum to lift heavy items into it. He gets tired and Mum puts him in the trolley.

This book uses a familiar context of shopping to present a simple structure with the item of shopping changing on each page. The position of change is easy to locate as it is at the end of a line of text. The items of shopping have frequently occurring letters that are easily distinguished. These characteristics make it a helpful early encounter with using initial letter information in text and tracking word by word.

Learning outcomes

Children can:

- understand that print carries meaning and is read from left to right, top to bottom
- use initial letter information to check understanding of picture information
- track two lines of simple repetitive text.

Developing reading comprehension

- The story is about Arif, even though the words tell us what Mum is doing.
- The reader needs to understand that the effort of helping Mum leads to Arif needing to be placed in the trolley at the end of the story.
- Children's previous experiences of toddlers being put in the trolley might be to keep them out of mischief so a full interpretation will need to be supported via discussion.

Grammar and sentence structure

- Text is well-spaced to support the development of one-to-one correspondence.
- Two lines of text on each page support the reinforcement of return sweep whilst tracking a slightly longer text.
- In contexts where children are learning English as an additional language, support by rehearsing the sentence structure orally before introducing the book.

Word meaning and spelling

- Check vocabulary predictions by attending to the first letter of nouns ('*apples*', '*oranges*', '*milk*', '*juice*', '*rice*', '*pizza*').
- Reinforce recognition of frequently occurring words ('*Mum*' '*in*' '*the*' '*puts*').

Curriculum Links

Maths – How much did each item of shopping cost? Maths investigations could calculate how much two or more ingredients cost, or work out how much change Arif could expect. Local currencies would provide the best context for this investigation.

Geography – What do we eat? Do Arif and Mum choose the same staple items as the children in your class? Or do they usually buy different things? This discussion could lead to creating block graphs to investigate which foods the children enjoy most.

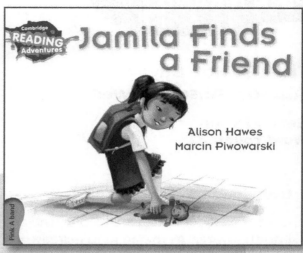

Title: Jamila Finds a Friend
Author: Alison Hawes

Genre: Fiction
Word count: 28

Overview

Jamila is on her way to school. She sees a series of things lying on the pavement: a book, a pencil, a ruler. Jamila picks them up. The trail continues until Jamila is able to return the items to their owner. The title draws attention to the fact that at this point a friendship begins.

The repeated sentence pattern has one change on each page. This change is supported by the clear illustration and serves to provide a context to begin to connect the words we speak and the letters we see.

Learning outcomes

Children can:

- understand that print carries meaning and is read from left to right
- attempt and practise one-to-one correspondence
- read a range of familiar and common sentences independently
- read and write a high-frequency word.

Developing reading comprehension

- This simple cumulative story supports development of early print concepts: that print carries meaning and is read from left to right.
- The use of the word 'finds' has a different meaning on the final page and this may need some discussion in second language learning contexts.

Grammar and sentence structure

- A simple one line repetitive sentence structure that includes the high-frequency word 'a' and introduces a new familiar, highly-redundant new word on each page.
- Some early opportunity to explore how punctuation aids expression when reading.

Word meaning and spelling

- Simple one-line text to attempt and practise one-to-one correspondence.
- Matching across a line of print, locating known words.
- Use of initial letter cues to cross-check with other information in print to problem-solve new words.

Curriculum links

Geography – Simple mapping of routes around the school or in the playground and what children find there.

Maths – Cumulative story. How many objects did Jamila find? What if she found two rulers? Three books?

Citizenship – Explore the nature of friendship. Who is your friend? Why are they your friend?

Title: A Hot Day
Author: Alison Hawes

Genre: Fiction
Word count: 42

Overview

It is hot in the jungle. One by one, the animals jump into the water. As the animals increase in size, so does the size of the splash. When Hippo jumps in, the rest of the animals get a soaking.

This humorous text provides a useful early experience with how print detail supports oral expression. As the word gets bigger, it should be read louder.

The name of the animal changes on every page. This creates a direct support for using letter information to inform reading.

Learning outcomes

Children can:

- turn pages appropriately
- understand that print is read from left to right
- match the spoken word to the printed word (one-to-one correspondence)
- locate known high frequency words in a line of text.

Developing reading comprehension

- Illustrations support the inference that as the animals get bigger, the impact on the pool of water will be greater. This may need to be drawn out through discussion.
- The animals in the story are commonly used in children's stories. Check that the names are known before reading the book so that the link between the vocabulary and the letter information is made clear.
- One line of text on a page provides the opportunity to practise early print concepts of directionality, one-to-one matching and location of known words.

Grammar and sentence structure

- One line of text offers just one word change, strongly supported by the illustrations.
- Simple punctuation, appearing at the same point on each page.

Word meaning and spelling

- High frequency words 'in' and 'the' repeated on each page.
- Large spaces between words to aid on-to-one matching across the line of text.

Curriculum links

Science and Nature – When Hippo jumps in, all the water splashes out! Use the water play area to explore water displacement: for example, how many bricks can we put in the pot before the water over-spills?

Title: Packing my Bag
Author: Alison Hawes

Genre: Fiction
Word count: 43

Overview

A bag is being packed for school. Each item needed for the day ahead is placed in the bag. It's time to go, friends are at the door. But something's missing! It's a wet day, but an umbrella has not been packed.

This text has a small number of high frequency words that appear in the same place in the sentence and on the page. This helps create a dependable environment to help the young reader begin to learn to look at print.

Learning outcomes

Children can:

- understand that print carries meaning and is read from left to right
- use initial letter information to check understanding of picture information
- track one line of simple repetitive text.

Developing reading comprehension

- The child in the book packs her bag for school, putting in the range of items that she will need for the day. One sentence structure is used throughout with a noun change on every page. This provides a consistent context for establishing control over one-to-one correspondence. On the final page, 'not' is inserted, requiring the reader to use both the meaning conveyed in the picture and simple print information.

Grammar and sentence structure

- Text is well-spaced to support the development of one-to-one correspondence.
- One line of text and highly predictable changes in the noun supported by clear illustrations.
- In contexts where children are learning English as an additional language, support by rehearsing the sentence structure orally before introducing the book.

Word meaning and spelling

- Check vocabulary predictions by attending to the first letter of nouns ('book', 'pen', 'ball', 'apple', 'lunch' 'drink', 'umbrella').
- Reinforce recognition of frequently occurring words 'my', 'is', 'in'.

Curriculum links

Language Development – Children could discuss the things they need for a day at school and share with the class how they prepare for school each day. This book links well to other Pink band texts in *Cambridge Reading Adventures* that deal with starting school and going to school ('Jamila Finds a Friend', 'Omar's First Day at School').

Maths – practical packing and unpacking activities would provide a good context for counting, counting on and conservation of number activities.

Title: Please Stop, Sara!
(Benchmark Text)
Author: Kathryn Harper

Genre: Fiction
Word count: 49

Overview

Sara is a young child with an interest in the world around her. As she plays around the house she finds a succession of things that make a noise or make a mess. Dad and Mum implore her to stop 'Please stop, Sara', but it takes Adam to restore calm. He finds a book and Sara settles down to listen to a story and cuddle up with Adam and Teddy.

The story provides a repeated sentence structure with a noun change on each page to begin to match spoken and writing language. The storyline provides additional support for the change on the last page from 'Please stop, Sara' to 'Don't stop, Adam.'

Learning outcomes

Children can:

- understand that print carries meaning and is read from left to right, top to bottom
- read some high-frequency words and use phonic knowledge to work out some simple regular words
- predict some plausible resolutions to this simple story
- track print across two lines of text.

Developing reading comprehension

- Everything Sara finds to play with causes a commotion, with family members asking 'Please stop, Sara' but Adam comes to the rescue and provides a solution. 'Don't stop, Adam!'.
- Simple repeated language patterns are used to convey this familiar family situation. Pictures are supportive of the story line.

Grammar and sentence structure

- Text is well-spaced to support the development of one-to-one correspondence.
- The position of the text supports the development of reading the left page before the right.

- The present tense is used to create a sense of action but this may need oral rehearsal before introducing the book in contexts where English is being learned as an additional language.

Word meaning and spelling

- Check vocabulary predictions by looking at the first letter of each item Sara finds ('drum', 'pot', 'car', 'duck', 'radio').
- Rehearse blending easy to hear sounds into a familiar word 'pot', 'stop'.
- Reinforce recognition of frequently occurring words 'the', 'stop'.

Curriculum links

PSHE – Adam tries very hard to look after Sara. Eventually, he holds the key to stopping the noise. What else might Adam do to help look after the troublesome toddler? Are any of the class older siblings? Can they report on what they do help to look after younger siblings?

Music – Explore everyday sounds. What has Sara got hold of now? Children could choose a toy or child's activity that makes a noise and play with it. The class has to guess what it is. Developing listening skills reinforces phonological awareness.

Title: Water
Author: Claire Llewellyn

Genre: Non-fiction
Word count: 35

Overview

This simple non-fiction report deals with the importance of water. Water is essential for plants to grow. This report lists some of them.

The nouns used are heavily supported by clear photographs. The changing noun is the first word in the sentence. This requires attention to the letter information unsupported by the syntactic redundancy offered by a language structure. Teaching needs to draw attention to how to check the letter information with the picture.

Learning outcomes

Children can:

- understand that print carries meaning and is read from left to right, top to bottom
- use initial letter information to check understanding of picture information
- identify capital letter forms.

Developing reading comprehension

- A direct language structure is used repetitively to create a non-fiction feel to this early text.
- Photographs provide support for the word change on every page.

Grammar and sentence structure

- Text is well-spaced to support the development of one-to-one correspondence.
- One line of text on each page provides a useful context for developing one-to-one correspondence and directional attention to print.
- In contexts where children are learning English as an additional language, support by rehearsing the sentence structure orally before introducing the book.

Word meaning and spelling

- Check vocabulary predictions by recognising that the words have capital letters as they start the sentence ('*Bananas*', '*Grapes*', '*Flowers*', '*Trees*', '*Apples*', '*Oranges*').
- Explain the particular context meaning of 'grow' in this text.
- Reinforce recognition of frequently occurring word '*to*'.

Curriculum links

Science and Nature – Plants need water to grow. But what else do we need water for? Shaping the level of information to match the age of the children, explore all the ways we need water for our everyday lives.

Geography – We need to conserve water whenever we can. Discuss ways that the children could contribute to this. Make posters and information sheets about conserving water in your specific context.

Title: The Sun is Up
Author: Claire Llewellyn

Genre: Non-fiction
Word count: 41

Overview

The sun is up! The sun's rays begin by reaching across the sea; then through the trees; onto the farm; on the pond. The sun's rays stretch as far as the town and then ultimately onto the child as she wakes.

The title is an oral language phrase that children may not be familiar with. As this sentence structure is not repeated in the book, there is no need to rehearse. It is more useful to return to the title after reading to locate the high frequency word 'The' and to locate 'sun', a word that appears frequently in this book.

Learning outcomes

Children can:

- demonstrate early book-handling skills
- understand that left page comes before right
- understand that print is read from left to right
- start to match spoken word to printed word (one-to-one correspondence) and confirm this matching using a few known words or letters
- work out the storyline by gathering information from the illustrations and repeated language patterns.

Developing reading comprehension

- Even though this simple explanatory text uses a repeated sentence structure, it has a non-literal meaning. When using this book, children need to be guided to the understanding that it is not the sun itself that is on the landscape, but its rays. This is supported by the illustrations throughout and it would be helpful to guide children to look at where the rays of sunlight are falling in order to gather information on the storyline.

Grammar and sentence structure

- One simple repeated sentence structure.
- Text is well-spaced to support the development of one-to-one correspondence.
- In contexts where children are learning English as an additional language, support by rehearsing the sentence structure orally before introducing the book.

Word meaning and spelling

- Rehearse blending easy to hear sounds into a familiar word 'sun'.
- Reinforce recognition of frequently occurring words 'The', 'on', 'the'.

Curriculum links

Science and Nature - This book provides useful links with the topic of the weather. The illustrations show the sun at different times of the day. This could be linked to science activities which chart the progression of the sun's rays during the day. The final page could be used to begin discussion on the harmful effects of the sun on skin.

Other Pink A texts in this series can be used to develop one-to-one correspondence.

Title: Games
Author: Lynne Rickards

Genre: Non-fiction
Word count: 29

Overview

A variety of games form this non-fiction report. Some of these games may be familiar to the young reader, others less so. Unfamiliar vocabulary needs to be prepared before reading this text so that the letter information can be used purposefully.

Learning outcomes

Children can:

- understand that print carries meaning and is read from left to right
- use initial letter information to check understanding of picture information
- track one line of simple repetitive text.

Developing reading comprehension

- This simple repetitive text is structured as a non-chronological report. One sentence structure is used to comment on a range of games that are enjoyed children the world over.

- The challenge includes the use of some games that are expressed in two words (for example, '*jump rope*') and some that are expressed in one (for example, '*hopscotch*', '*dress-up*'). The children have to match what is said with what they see very carefully to maintain one-to-one correspondence.

Grammar and sentence structure

- Text is well-spaced to support the development of one-to-one correspondence.

- One line of text and highly predictable changes in the noun supported by clear illustrations.

- In contexts where children are learning English as an additional language, support by rehearsing the sentence structure orally before introducing the book.

Word meaning and spelling

- Check vocabulary predictions by attending to letter information ('*marbles*', '*chess*', '*football*', '*jump rope*', '*hopscotch*', '*dress-up*', '*games*').

- Reinforce recognition of frequently occurring words '*I*', '*like*', '*playing*'.

Curriculum links

Language Development – Many of the games pictured in the book have rules or an accepted way to play. Children could provide explanations of how to play the games. Vocabulary of sequence and order (first, next, then, for example) can be developed in contexts. Some children may need support to sequence their thinking and talking. This could be done by picture cards or by using the games equipment itself.

Maths – which games do the children prefer? Simple tally charts and surveys could provide the numbers to make some simple graphs and charts.

Title: Animal Homes
Author: Lauri Kubuitsile

Genre: Non-fiction
Word count: 56

Overview

The non-fiction context uses a series of clear photographs to show the reader where a variety of animals make their homes.

The change on each page is supported by photographs. This text is useful to develop use of letter information to check oral prediction. The natural language patterns support help the learner to expect words to match the text.

Learning outcomes

Children can:

- understand that print carries meaning and is read from left to right, top to bottom
- use initial letter information to check understanding of picture information
- track two lines of simple repetitive text.

Developing reading comprehension

- This simple, repetitive text is set in a non-fiction context. The natural language structure helps the learner to expect words to match the text.
- Two simple sentences are used to inform the reader about where animals make their homes. The names for the homes may be unfamiliar to some children reading this book.

Grammar and sentence structure

- Text is well-spaced to support the development of one-to-one correspondence.
- Two lines of text on each page support the reinforcement of return sweep whilst tracking a slightly longer text.
- In contexts where children are learning English as an additional language, support by rehearsing the sentence structure orally before introducing the book.

Word meaning and spelling

- Check vocabulary predictions by attending to the first letter of the nouns ('den', 'shell', 'pond', 'web', 'cave', 'hole').
- Reinforce recognition of frequently occurring words ('Look', 'in', 'me', 'I', 'at', 'a').

Curriculum links

Nature – Habitats provide animals with food or shelter. Discuss how the habitats in this text are important. 'A House for Snail' (Yellow band) would make a useful fiction link to the idea of an ideal home for every creature.

Geography – Where do we live? Create and collect photos and pictures of the type of homes and houses that the children live in. These can be displayed with simple captions and labels to name the types of housing. 'Houses and Homes' (Red band) could be shared with the children as a model.

Title: Photos
Author: Alison Hawes

Genre: Fiction
Word count: 29

Overview

In a humorous twist to a familiar setting, this story with a repetitive structure features a little girl trying to take some photos of her family, but the parrot keeps getting in the way of all her attempts to compose a good shot on the tablet.

Learning outcomes

Children can:

- understand that print carries meaning and is read from left to right
- develop awareness of capital letter forms.
- track one line of simple repetitive text.

Developing reading comprehension

- Strong links between the text and supportive illustrations support children to make sense of what they are reading.
- Humour and familiarity with the family setting make this an easily accessible to young children.

Grammar and sentence structure

- Text is well-spaced to support the development of one-to-one correspondence. The addition of 'And' on the final page creates a subtle challenge to self-monitoring of one-to-one correspondence.
- A repetitive sentence structure is used to tell the story. Highly predictable changes in the noun are supported by clear illustrations.
- In contexts where children are learning English as an additional language, support by rehearsing the sentence structure orally before introducing the book.

Word meaning and spelling

- Use letter information to check use of familiar use of vocabulary (*Grandpa, Grandma*).
- Reinforce recognition of frequently occurring words *Here is my*

Curriculum links

Literacy – Plan a menu for the barbecue in the garden, presenting the items in a list. Children could then illustrate the list. This activity could be done as a class, in small groups or as an individual task.

Language development – Ask the children to retell the story using the same sentence structure (Here is my …) with members of their own family and substituting a different animal that keeps getting in the camera shot. The animal chosen for this oracy activity can be chosen to fit the specific context.

Title: The Tractor
Author: Alison Hawes

Genre: Fiction
Word count: 35

Overview

The family have arrived for a day's visit to the farm. They are looking forward to having an exciting day and seeing lots of animals. But it looks like the bad weather is going to spoil their plans, until the tractor comes to help.

Learning outcomes

Children can:

- understand that print carries meaning and is read from left to right

- use initial letter information to check understanding of picture information

- track one line of simple repetitive text.

Developing reading comprehension

- The illustrations support the story line, with the oncoming rain storm shown progressively across events.

- Opportunity for prediction and problem-solving, as the children think about the family's predicament.

Grammar and sentence structure

- Text is well-spaced to support the development of one-to-one correspondence.

- One repeated sentence structure uses high frequency words, with a change to the noun on each page. This is supported by clear illustrations and the placement of the noun in the sentence.

- Punctuation is changed to an exclamation mark on the last page to support the meaning information

Word meaning and spelling

- Use letter information to check vocabulary choice ('farm', 'goats', 'cows', 'chickens', 'rain" 'mud', 'tractor').

- Reinforce recognition of frequently occurring words *We can see the*

Curriculum links

Geography – The children in the book experience a day on the farm. Explore the range of food people get from farms: crops, dairy and meat.

Science and Maths – The rain comes and makes the road muddy. Set up a mud kitchen experiment and see what happens to earth and sand when water is added. Use a variety of containers to experiment with different amounts of water.

Title: I Can Help
Author: Lynne Rickards

Genre: Fiction
Word count: 42

Overview

This non-chronological report uses a simple sentence structure to report on a variety of ways in which children across the world can help. Some of the names of the locations pictured are multisyllabic words (for example, *'library, classroom, kitchen*). This presents a challenge to the young reader who may expect there to be a space between each syllable. Monitoring one-to-one correspondence is key to the effective use of this simple text.

Learning outcomes

Children can:

- understand that print carries meaning and is read from left to right
- use initial letter information to check understanding of picture information
- track one line of simple repetitive text.

Developing reading comprehension

- Strong links between children's own experiences and those featured in the book.

Grammar and sentence structure

- Text is well-spaced to support the development of one-to-one correspondence.
- One line of text and highly predictable changes in the noun supported by clear illustrations.
- In contexts where children are learning English as an additional language, support by rehearsing the sentence structure orally before introducing the book.

Word meaning and spelling

- Attending to letter information supports the reading of new vocabulary words (*'garden'*, *'market'*, *'barn'*, *'shop'*, *' kitchen'*, *'classroom'*, *'library'*).
- Reinforce recognition of frequently occurring words *I, can, help, in, the*

Curriculum links

Social Studies – The books shows some ways that children can help. How do children in your class help? How do they help other children? How do they help adults? Discussion on ways the children can help other people could be followed by illustrating some of the ways that the class help others.

Language development – Using pictures, develop vocabulary of everyday situations. For example, rooms in the home, places we visit, such as library, supermarket, bakery, park. For each place, discuss some ways in which we might help other people.

Title: My Dad is a Builder
Author: Lynne Rickards

Genre: Fiction
Word count: 63

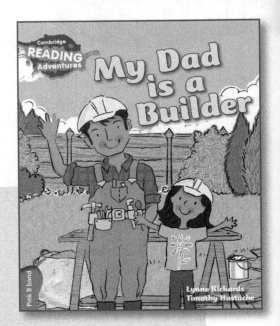

Overview

Dad is building something. Each tool is revealed in turn. The question is repeated on each page to emphasise the idea that it is not clear what Dad is building. On the final page, the secret is revealed. Dad is building a playhouse.

The repeated question provides an opportunity to rehearse oral reading expression supported by a clear meaning and a distinctive natural language phrase.

Learning outcomes

Children can:

- use some letters together with meaning to read the text

- match spoken to printed word (one-to-one correspondence) across 2 lines of print and confirm this matching using a few known words

- show some awareness of mismatches between reading attempts and the printed text

- work out the storyline by gathering information from the illustrations and repeated language patterns.

Developing reading comprehension

- This simple one-line text provides opportunity for children to attempt and practise one-to-one correspondence.

- The use of a question *'What is my dad building?'* indicates that reading is about making sense of what is being read. Teachers can support this through prompting and questioning as more information is provided as the text progresses.

Grammar and sentence structure

- A simple two-line repetitive sentence structure well-supported by the illustrations.

- Recognition of punctuation (question mark) to aid fluency of expression at this early band.

Word meaning and spelling

- Matching across a line of print, locating and reading known high frequency words: *'my'*, *'is'*, *'Dad'*.

- Use of initial letter cues to cross-check with other information in print to problem-solve new words.

- Introduce new high frequency word *'some'*.

Curriculum links

Art – Children plan, design and build their own house.

Geography – Homes in different parts of the world. Link with other books in *Cambridge Reading Adventures* (e.g. 'Houses and Homes' Red band). In 'Omar Can Help' (Yellow band), Omar helps his friends build a house.

Title: The Last Lemon
Author: Alison Hawes

Genre: Fiction
Word count: 75

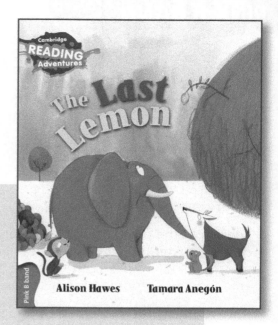

Overview

The last lemon is high up in a tree. How will Elephant get it? His animal friends come to help and climb on top of each other so that the last lemon can be reached.

The repeated language structures extend across two pages. The young reader needs to rely less on oral memory and more on the words and letters that they know.

Learning outcomes

Children can:

- understand that print carries meaning and is read from left to right, top to bottom
- read some high-frequency words and use phonic knowledge to work out some simple words
- show an understanding of the sequence of events.

Developing reading comprehension

- Elephant can't reach the last lemon, so he gets help from his friends. This humorous story builds up using three language structures repeated across several pages. This challenges the reader to follow the story meaning and notice the changes in use of vocabulary.
- Understanding and noticing the change between 'can' and 'can't' is important when using this book.

Grammar and sentence structure

- Text is well-spaced to support the development of one-to-one correspondence and return sweep onto a new line of text.
- In contexts where children are learning English as an additional language, support by rehearsing the sentence structures orally before introducing the book.

Word meaning and spelling

- Check vocabulary predictions by looking at the first letter of each animal.
- Rehearse blending easy to hear sounds into a familiar word 'can', 'get'.
- Reinforce recognition of frequently occurring words 'said', 'the', 'I'.

Curriculum links

Design and Technology - The idea of building a tall structure can be linked to design and technology work where children can explore making towers using a variety of construction toys and junk modelling activities.

Other Pink B texts in this series can be used to develop reading two lines of text on a page and beginning to use a greater variety of simple language structures.

Title: Leela can Skate
Author: Alison Hawes

Genre: Fiction
Word count: 38

Overview

Leela is at the park with her brother. She practises skating by demonstrating all the things she can do on her skates. She can put them on, stand up, run, spin, hop. But stopping is not so easy!

Attention to print is needed to notice that 'stand up' requires careful tracking. The introduction of the word 'Help' on the last page is supported by the storyline.

Learning outcomes

Children can:

- understand that print carries meaning and is read from left to right, top to bottom
- read some high-frequency words and use phonic knowledge to work out some simple words
- show an understanding of a sequence of events.

Developing reading comprehension

- Leela is learning to skate. But she can't stop. Simple language structures are used repetitively to explain what she can and can't do on her skates.
- Pictures provide good support for the text meaning.

Grammar and sentence structure

- Text is well-spaced to support the development of one-to-one correspondence.
- The changes to two lines of text on pages 12-13, provide good support for early experiences of return sweep onto a new line of text.
- In contexts where children are learning English as an additional language, support by rehearsing the sentence structures orally before introducing the book.

Word meaning and spelling

- Check vocabulary predictions by looking at the first letter of each action ('*jump*', '*run*', '*hop*', '*stand up*').
- Rehearse blending easy to hear sounds into a familiar word '*can*', '*run*'.
- Reinforce recognition of frequently occurring words '*put*', '*on*', '*my*'.

Curriculum links

PSHE – Leela wears shin pads, knee pads and a helmet throughout. Why does she wear them? What other play activities do the children need to wear protective clothing to do?

Science and Nature – Explore a selection of everyday objects to find out which can roll. Grouping and sorting activities would support discussion and practical investigations. Why do they roll? Do they have particular spatial properties?

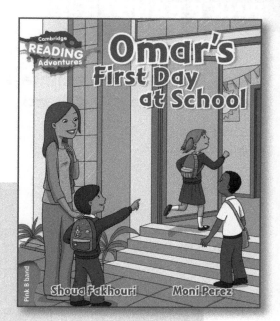

Title: Omar's First Day at School
Author: Shoua Fakhouri

Genre: fiction
Word count: 57

Overview

This is the first story in the International School strand of *Cambridge Reading Adventures*. It is Omar's first day at school. Lots of things are new. He introduces Mum to his teacher and to his new friends.

This is a familiar experience to all children. The language in the book helps increase reading experience with some common sentence structures. The change in sentence structure involves two common high frequency words ('*is*' and '*are*') and helps beginning to move away from relying on oral memory to read.

Learning outcomes

Children can:

- locate the title, open the book and turn pages appropriately

- recognise mismatches between their reading attempts and the printed text

- identify and read known high frequency words in multiple lines of text.

Developing reading comprehension

- This is a familiar experience for all young children and will support their comprehension of this simple Pink B band text.

Grammar and sentence structure

- A repetitive whole-sentence structure, mirroring children's natural language patterns.

- Two or three lines of text requiring directional and word-matching skills.

- A change from 3rd person singular to 3rd person plural on the last page, from '*This is ...*' to '*Beno and Zara are ...*'

Word meaning and spelling

- Repetition of high frequency words: '*This*', '*is*', '*my*', '*said*'.

- The changing noun on each page is strongly supported by illustrations, and by recognition of the initial letter.

Curriculum links

PSHE – What could help make a new child's first day at school easier? The class could think of all the new things that a new entrant will encounter and write some advice or guidance for a welcome leaflet.

Title: Our Den (Benchmark Text)
Author: Gabby Pritchard

Genre: Fiction
Word count: 87

Overview

Sami and Max work together to make a den. Sami fetches the things they need, whilst Max gives his approval to each new improvement to the den. They end up with a den to be proud of.

This text has two to four lines of text on a page and offers a context in which to assess control of one-to-one correspondence within a repetitive sentence structure.

The change between 'a' and 'some' may be challenging for second-language learners who may not predict the change in structure needed for the plural/singular nouns. It is useful to develop close attention to print.

The relationship between the two boys reinforces the relative size and implied age. However, the younger child is portrayed positively. Max takes the lead, but Sami made the den.

Learning outcomes

Children can:

- understand that print carries meaning and, is read from left to right, top to bottom
- use initial letter information to check understanding of picture information
- track two to four lines of simple repetitive text.

Developing reading comprehension

- Three sentence structures provide high challenge at Pink B as the reader has to be able to track left to right and return over four lines of text.
- This relationship reinforces the relative size and implied age of the two boys. The younger child is portrayed positively and he contributes usefully.

Grammar and sentence structure

- Text is well-spaced to support the development of one-to-one correspondence.
- Two to four lines of text consolidate and challenge return sweep on text with longer sentence structures.
- In contexts where children are learning English as an additional language, support by rehearsing the sentence structure orally before introducing the book.

Word meaning and spelling

- Check vocabulary predictions by attending to the first letter of nouns ('blankets', 'string', 'pegs', 'table', 'chairs' 'food').
- Reinforce recognition of frequently occurring words ('for', 'some', 'said', 'the', 'got', 'Look').

Curriculum links

Language Development – Make a class den using string, pegs and blankets, just like Sami and Max. This could be used as a reading den; children could sit on cushions to read a range of their favourite texts and maybe add some soft toys.

Develop the use of instructional language by putting children in the role of leader, providing instructions as to what to do next to form the den.

Title: Looking After Animals
Author: Claire Llewellyn

Genre: Non-fiction
Word count: 64

Overview

In this book, the need to care for animals is introduced. A link is made between what animals need and how we need to care for them.

By using the language of a non-chronological report, the context is created to pay close attention to print. The text has many opportunities to recognise high frequency words introduced in earlier texts ('*We*', '*to*', '*the*', '*a*', '*look*').

Learning outcomes

Children can:

- attend to print detail, including one-to-one matching across a line of text
- read some high-frequency words
- use phonic knowledge to work out some simple words.

Developing reading comprehension

- Simple text with a repetitive structure and familiar content.
- Features of an early non-chronological report through the inclusion of photographs and in referring to generic participants ('*cats*', '*donkeys*'), rather than specific participants – 'this donkey', 'my cat', for example.

Grammar and sentence structure

- Three whole-sentence structures across the book each including at least one high frequency word.
- Simple punctuation (capital letters and full stops) occurs in the same position on each page.

Word meaning and spelling

- The changing nouns and verbs on each page are strongly supported by illustrations, and by recognition of the initial letter.
- A number of familiar high frequency words are included to aid development of fast, fluent reading, even at this early band.

Curriculum links

Science and Nature – Caring for school pets or creatures in the school wildlife garden would provide a good link with this book. The book could also support studies of different animal habitats – see 'Animal Homes' (Pink A band in *Cambridge Reading Adventures*).

PSHE – A topic on people who help could include vets and others who care for animals.

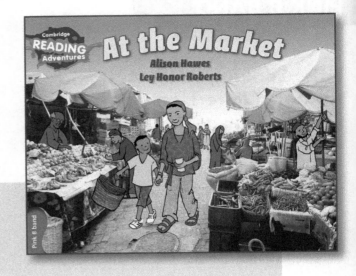

Title: At the Market
Author: Alison Hawes

Genre: Non-fiction
Word count: 45

Overview

A boy and his mother visit the market to do some shopping. They visit different market stalls to buy what they need for dinner. They buy fish, spices, vegetables, fruit and rice.

Three language structures are used across the book to report on what they buy. Some simple labels of words in the text are used.

Learning outcomes

Children can:

- understand that print carries meaning and is read from left to right, top to bottom
- read some high-frequency words and use phonic knowledge to work out some simple words
- show an understanding of the sequence of events
- indicate how information can be found in non-fiction text.

Developing reading comprehension

- This cumulative text shows parent and child visiting a local market to buy food for dinner. The pictures are colourful and provide lots of scope for discussion and comparison with local context. The meal at the end of the book is made from the ingredients gathered during the trip to the market.
- The change in language structure on alternate pages may be challenging for children learning English as an additional language and requires support by rehearsing the sentence structure orally before introducing the book.

Grammar and sentence structure

- Support the change in language structure by attending to letter information 'buy'/'buys'.

Word meaning and spelling

- Check vocabulary predictions by checking the first letter of the food bought at the market.
- Rehearse blending easy to hear sounds into familiar words 'go' and 'at'.
- Reinforce recognition of frequently occurring words 'the' 'to'

Curriculum links

Maths – The context of buying food can link to practical mathematics activities with weight and money: How much did each thing bought at the market cost? How much does it cost to buy vegetables and spices? Which is heavier; the fish or the rice?

Cookery – Discussion of the meal could be developed into cookery activities in school or collecting favourite recipes from the cultures represented by the children.

Language development – Set up a shop or market play area in the classroom for the children to reinforce the language structures, vocabulary and concepts of the book in their play activities.

Other Pink B texts in this series can be used to develop one-to-one correspondence across small changes in language structure.

Title: Who Lays Eggs?
Author: Claire Llewellyn

Genre: Non-fiction
Word count: 106

Overview

This non-fiction report provides information on a clear topic. Animals hide their eggs to keep them safe. This text shows the reader some of the many places that animals use to keep their eggs safe. Some of the vocabulary is used in unfamiliar ways. For example, the nest a wasp uses to keep its eggs safe may not be familiar to young children.

Learning outcomes

Children can:

- know that print carries meaning and is read from left to right, top to bottom

- read some high-frequency words and use phonic knowledge to work out some simple words

- indicate how information can be found in non-fiction text.

Developing reading comprehension

- This text works in a different way to a story and has simple captions of the names of the animals. Children need to be guided to understand that the text refers to generic groups – all lizards, for example, not just the one in the illustration.

- Three language structures are used on each page. Tracking three lines of text may be challenging for some so rehearsing tracking and return sweep across three lines of text needs to be secured as part of introducing the book.

Grammar and sentence structure

- Support the change in vocabulary by attending to letter information ('*soil*', '*nest*', '*log*').

- Reinforce use of the pronoun 'it' to refer to the animal being discussed.

Word meaning and spelling

- Check knowledge of technical vocabulary '*lays*', '*soil*', '*log*', '*nest*', '*leaf*'.

- Rehearse blending easy to hear sounds into familiar words '*in*' '*eggs*'.

- Reinforce recognition of frequently occurring words '*are*' '*the*' '*A*'.

Curriculum links

Science and Nature – The information in this book could be used as part of classroom activities in science and nature to discuss mammals/ non-mammals or characteristics of egg-laying animals (some are reptiles, some are birds, some are fish, for example). These animals have developed ways of keeping their young safe. Children could use other texts to inform making charts of predators and prey.

Other Pink B texts in this series can be used to develop one-to-one correspondence and tracking across 2-3 lines of text.

Title: Where do they Grow?
Author: Lynne Rickards

Genre: Non-fiction
Word count: 63

Overview

This non-fiction report uses a question and answer structure to present where some widely-used fruit and vegetables grow.

Although text placement is consistent, an additional challenge is placed on use of return sweep as now a picture separates the question and answer sentence structures.

Learning outcomes

Children can:

- understand that print carries meaning and is read from left to right, top to bottom
- use initial letter information to check word choice
- use picture information and known letters to inform reading for the precise meaning and to discriminate between 'in' and 'on'
- track two lines of simple repetitive text.

Developing reading comprehension

- Two structures are used repetitively throughout the book. One of those structures is a question and so the use of the question mark to inform expression.
- Children who live in cities and towns may not see food being grown. In this instance, discuss how the fruit and vegetables we eat are grown and that they may grow on trees or bushes in the ground.
- The high frequency words 'in' and 'on' are used with a specific meaning in this text.

Grammar and sentence structure

- Text is well-spaced to support the development of one-to-one correspondence.
- Two lines of text on each page support the reinforcement of return sweep whilst tracking a slightly longer text.

- In contexts where children are learning English as an additional language, support by rehearsing the sentence structure orally before introducing the book.

Word meaning and spelling

- The prepositions ('on', 'in') change depending on the context of each page.
- The nouns are used with lower case and capital letters, depending on their position in the sentence.

Curriculum links

Mathematics – Use pictures of fruit and vegetables to sort into sets according to where they grow.

Science and Nature – Cress, beansprouts and lentils can be grown in the classroom. This could lead to investigations. What do they need to grow? Light? Water? Where in the classroom do they grow best?

PINK B BAND

Title: Hello, Baby
Author: Glen Franklin and Sue Bodman

Genre: Fiction
Word count: 42

Overview

Everyone in the family tries to stop Baby crying, but nothing they try seems to work. Even Teddy can't help. The only one who can make her happy is her Granddad.

Learning outcomes

Children can:

- understand that print carries meaning and is read from left to right, top to bottom;
- read some high-frequency words
- Use phonic knowledge to decode simple words

Developing reading comprehension

- Relationships in families can be explored through this simple premise.
- Discussion about why the baby might be crying could reinforce comprehension and exploit children's prior knowledge of babies and younger siblings.

Grammar and sentence structure

- Text is well-spaced to support the development of one-to-one correspondence.
- Two lines of text reinforce return sweep onto a new line of text.
- The use of the present tense throughout ('says' rather than 'said', 'cries' instead of 'cried') gives the story a sense of immediacy.

Word meaning and spelling

- Check vocabulary predictions by looking at the first letter of each character's names (*Mum, Dad, Gran, Grandad*)
- Rehearse blending easy to hear sounds into a simple name *Sam Ben*
- Use of capital letters for names

Curriculum links

Language Development – The story context will be familiar to children with younger siblings. Ask the children to bring in pictures of when they were a baby. Each child can tell the rest of the class what made them laugh or smile when they were a baby.

Drama – Facial expressions are an important method of social communication. Ask the children to work in pairs and enact a target emotion – happy, sad, angry, surprise. For slightly older children, more subtle emotions could be included – boredom, disgust, pride. Children could take pictures of themselves and write simple sentences about what they might be thinking about when experiencing these emotions.

Title: School Lunch
Author: Glen Franklin and Sue Bodman

Genre: Fiction
Word count: 38

Overview

It is lunch time at school. A small boy queues up and requests the things he wants for lunch. But as he walks to his table, an accident occurs! He spills his milk and has to ask for another drink.

Learning outcomes

Children can:

- understand that print carries meaning and is read from left to right, top to bottom
- read some high-frequency words
- show an understanding of the sequence of events.

Developing reading comprehension

- The familiar setting of a school lunch room will support children to empathise with the little boy's predicament.
- The food he chooses to eat will be familiar to most children across different regions and contexts.

Grammar and sentence structure

- Text is well-spaced to support the development of one-to-one correspondence.
- The position of the text on each page is clear and supportive of understanding to read the left page before the right.

- A question structure is repeated on each page with a change in noun. 'Please' is located on a new line, supporting the phrasing of a question.

Word meaning and spelling

- Check vocabulary predictions by looking at the first letter ('rice', 'chicken', 'salad', 'fruit', 'milk').
- Using a simple repeated question structure
- Reinforce recognition of frequently occurring words Can, I, have, some.

Curriculum links

Science – A blind food tasting activity will encourage language to describe taste and temperature; warm/cold; sweet/sour; hard/soft.

Geography – What is on offer for lunch at school today? How does this compare with other children in another part of the world?

Title: Where Are You Going?
Author: Glen Franklin and Sue Bodman

Genre: Fiction
Word count: 69

Overview

A simple question and answer structure is adopted for this cumulative story in which Ana sees a series of interesting looking characters pass by her window. Where are they going? Luckily, Ana gets to join her father at the carnival celebrations!

Learning outcomes

Children can:

- understand that print carries meaning and is read from left to right, top to bottom

- read some high-frequency words and use phonic knowledge to work out some simple regular words

- show an understanding of the sequence of events.

Developing reading comprehension

- The real reason for the people passing by is revealed on the final pages as Ana gets to go to the carnival herself. Children will be encouraged to predict this outcome as they read through the book.

Grammar and sentence structure

- Text is well-spaced to support the development of one-to-one correspondence.

- The position of the text on each page is clear and supportive of understanding to read the left page before the right, top before bottom.

- The present tense and a reporting clause are used.

- The preposition 'to' to start a sentence is used to create a natural language interaction; this may need oral rehearsal as part of the book introduction in contexts where English is being learned as an additional language.

Word meaning and spelling

- Check vocabulary predictions by looking at the first letter of each character Ana sees (boy, girl, man, woman).

- Using a simple repeated question structure and question mark

- Reinforce recognition of frequently occurring words *said, the, you, going*

Curriculum links

Art – Make some carnival headdresses. Children could look at a range of pictures and choose the type of headdress they want to make. Alternatively, local customs and celebration could provide the stimulus for this creative activity.

Music – The carnival has musicians and dancers. Use a range of percussion instruments to play a carnival beat together. The activity would involve listening carefully to rhythms and repeating them in a question and answer style.

Title: Bedtime on the Farm
Author: Alex Eeles

Genre: Fiction
Word count: 102

Overview

On the farm, Dev wants to put the animals to bed. But where are they? The animals need persuading with a little treat.

The storyline lends itself to repetition of phrases, supporting reading with phrasing and expression. In Red band, the phrase patterns are not repeated on every page and there are frequent changes to reflect the storyline. This requires sustained attention to print.

Learning outcomes

Children can:

- use punctuation to inform phrasing and expression
- use phonic knowledge to solve new and unfamiliar words
- comment on the events and characters in the story, making links to other stories.

Developing reading comprehension

- Strong support from the illustrations provides good opportunities to begin to call for phrased reading and interpretation of the story.
- High frequency words feature highly in the sentence structures to continue to build word recognition.

Grammar and sentence structure

- The repetition of sentences and phrases across up to four lines of text consolidates one-to-one correspondence and return sweep.
- Begin to read smoothly and using a finger to track at points of difficulty only.
- The use of 'says' may be unfamiliar to many children, and needs supporting prior to reading.

Word meaning and spelling

- Opportunity to rehearse and read a wide range of known high frequency words.
- Practise and consolidation of regular decodable words.

Curriculum links

Maths – This story shows a night-time routine on the farm. Children could discuss the tasks that need doing on a farm and sort them into Day/Night or to extend the level of challenge, Morning/Afternoon/Evening/Night. Links could be made with other time-sequenced stories.

PSHE – Dev looks after the animals on the farm. What do the children do to look after animals in their homes and communities? 'Looking after Animals' (Pink B band) could be reread to add to this discussion.

Title: Leopard and his Spots
Author: Kathryn Harper

Genre: Fiction
Word count: 88

Overview

At the opening of the story, Leopard looked at his own reflection and decided that he didn't like his spots. He visited the doctor who tried to help him by giving him all sorts of remedies, all of which have disastrous effects. Leopard was happy to have his spots back!

The repetitive nature of the story aids reading for meaning and thinking about the plot development as a source of information. The range of punctuation supports the development of phrased and fluent reading, but the subtle changes in plural/singular demand attention to print detail.

Learning outcomes

Children can:

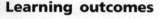

- solve simple words by sounding out and blending phonemes left to right and checking that what they say looks right and makes sense
- use known words, including irregular high-frequency words, to check and confirm meaning
- read in a more phrased manner while maintaining track of the print.

Developing reading comprehension

- The highly predictable text and the refrain 'Oh no!' support reading with expression and comprehension.

Grammar and sentence structure

- Simple repeated sentence structures with changes supported by the illustrations.
- Some punctuated speech aids phrased and expressive reading.
- Opportunity to consolidate directionality and one-to-one correspondence across two lines of text and across a two-page spread.

Word meaning and spelling

- Opportunity to rehearse regular phonically decodable CVC words ('red', 'him', 'yes'), and to consolidate known high frequency words ('said', 'the', 'like').
- Early exploration of elision in the word 'didn't' to mirror natural language pattern.
- The change in structure from 'Oh no!' said the doctor.' to 'Yes!' said Leopard.' requires focused attention to print detail.

Curriculum links

Art – Children could create their fantastical Leopard using scrap material – what might they use for his fur?

Literacy – Read other stories where people or animals are unhappy with their appearance, such as 'Elmer the Elephant' or 'The Rainbow Fish'.

Title: The Enormous Watermelon
Author: Alison Hawes

Genre: Fiction
Word count: 107

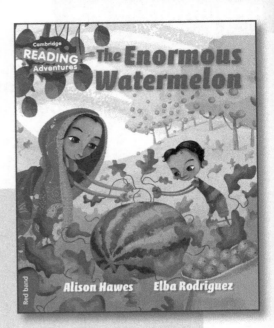

Overview

Mum and Ravi pick an enormous watermelon. How can they carry it to market? Ravi sees a wheelbarrow and has a good idea. Thanks to clever Ravi, they get to market. But they don't manage to sell the enormous watermelon. This time it's Mum that has the good idea. She cuts the watermelon into slices and they manage to sell it all. Clever Mum!

Learning outcomes

Children can:

- solve simple words by blending phonemes from left to right and check for meaning, correct syntax i.e. does it make sense and sound right?
- locate and read high frequency words
- show an understanding of the elements of stories
- start to read in a more phrased manner while maintaining track of the print.

Developing reading comprehension

- Mum and Ravi work together to solve the problem of the enormous watermelon. The story parallels other familiar and traditional tales about fruit or vegetables that grow larger than the norm and are hard to harvest.

Grammar and sentence structure

- Repetition of phrases and a recurring theme support the reading.
- Text features such as bold text and punctuation support phrased and expressive reading.

Word meaning and spelling

- Opportunity to rehearse and recognize known words in context.
- Longer words such as 'watermelon' and 'wheelbarrow' can be used to demonstrate location of known items which can be used to solve unfamiliar words.

Curriculum links

Maths - The story lends itself to mathematics activities on division and fractions. How many people could buy a slice of watermelon if it was cut in different ways?

Citizenship - Explore the theme of sharing and how everyone was able to have a piece of the melon. 'Omar Can Help' (Yellow band) also has the theme of sharing.

Title: Omar can Help
Author: Lynne Rickards

Genre: Fiction
Word count: 114

Overview

Omar is good at helping. He helps Zara and Leila make their house. He helps Beno build a tower that will stand up without wobbling. But when Omar tries to help Kofi as Zara shares a cake, he jumps up to get a plate and falls over. Now he is the one who needs help. And his friends do not let him down.

Learning outcomes

Children can:

- read simple words by sounding out and blending phonemes left to right
- use syntax and context when reading for meaning
- locate, read, and write high-frequency words.

Developing reading comprehension

- This is a story about Omar and his friends. Omar is keen to help but often his best intentions go wrong. Inference is needed to understand the actions illustrated on pages 10 and 11. Omar is going to share his own cake with Kofi. He slips on a banana skin. Neither of these facts are in the text and so the reader has to use illustrations and context to understand.

Grammar and sentence structure

- Simple sentence structures repeated in different contexts.
- Repetition of spoken phrases and punctuated speech to aid expression and reading for meaning.

Word meaning and spelling

- Opportunity to rehearse regular phonically decodable words ('*can*', '*help*', '*stick*').
- Vowel digraph /*ew*/
- Explore compound words ('*everyone*', '*outside*')

Curriculum links

Mathematics – Zara brought a cake to share. How would she divide it up to ensure there was a piece for everyone?

Design and Technology – Omar helped the girls fix the roof of their house. Explore ways of building different roof shapes.

RED BAND

Title: Seagull
Author: Kathryn Harper

Genre: Fiction
Word count: 76

Overview

In this simple story, Seagull encounters various pollutants which make her increasingly unrecognisable. Pep and Lin find Seagull and are at first unsure what sort of creature they have encountered. The two children help each other to clean Seagull up. Then they contribute to the task of cleaning up the beach.

Although the language structures are simple, speech sometimes continues over two lines of text, requiring the reader to pay close attention to speech punctuation and full stops to read with the appropriate phrasing and juncture. The topic is serious, despite the humorous-looking figures and the potential humour in Seagull being covered in rags and litter. Understanding that this is not a funny story requires the reader to interpret using both words and illustrations.

Learning outcomes

Children can:

- control accurate one-to-one matching over one or two short lines of text
- sound out simple words and blend phonemes from left to right
- read a range of short sentences independently and with expression.

Developing reading comprehension

- Children need to understand that the dirt and rags that Seagull encounters are the result of human activity. This explains the final page spread where other also help to clean up the beach.

Grammar and sentence structure

- Short, clear, and straightforward sentences that following children's natural language.
- Some punctuated speech requires phrased and expressive reading.
- Repetitive clause patterns including use of adverbial phrases ('*into the water*'; '*onto the beach*').

Word meaning and spelling

- Simple words ('*Pep*', '*Lin*', '*can*', '*help*') that children can solve by blending phonemes.
- Opportunity to rehearse known high frequency words together in context, such as '*Look at me*'.

Curriculum links

Art – The artist has used collage techniques to create the pictures in this book. Children could create their own collage pictures of Pep, Lin and Seagull on the beach.

PSHE – Whilst pollution itself may be a rather advanced topic for six and seven year olds, children could devise a 'Keep Our School Tidy' campaign, with posters in areas of the school that can become untidy.

58

Title: Look! It's Baby Duck (Benchmark Text)
Author: Gabby Pritchard

Genre: Fiction
Word count: 64

Overview

Brown Mouse and Grey Mouse are out for a walk when they come across a baby duck. Intrigued, they follow to see what he can do. They watch on as Baby Duck practises swimming, walking, quacking and flying. But Baby Duck has the last laugh. Just as Grey Mouse is thinking about whether Baby Duck can play, Baby Duck shows that he can by jumping up behind them and shouting 'Boo!'.

Learning outcomes

Children can:

- solve simple words by blending phonemes from left to right and check for meaning, correct syntax i.e. does it make sense and sound right?
- locate and read high-frequency words
- show an understanding of the elements of stories
- start to read in a more phrased manner while maintaining track of the print.

Developing reading comprehension

- Brown Mouse and Grey Mouse find out that Baby Duck can do many things – including surprising them when they get too close.

Grammar and sentence structure

- A simple repeated sentence structure with well-placed changes support the consolidation of one-to-one correspondence across three lines of text on a page.
- Bold text and punctuation support phrased and expressive reading.

Word meaning and spelling

- Opportunity to rehearse and recognise frequently occurring words in context – 'said', 'can', 'Look', 'He'
- The change in structure to 'shouted' gives the opportunity to look closely at print detail.

Curriculum links

Physical Education – Following simple instructions to change movement – walk, jump, hop, run.

PSHE – charting the changes that we undergo from baby, to toddler, to child.

Title: Our Senses
Author: Claire Llewellyn

Genre: Non-fiction
Word count: 100

Overview

What can we do with our senses? This non-fiction text provides support for learning about how we use our five senses in everyday life. A clear chart sets out the information graphically so that children can begin to use information displayed in tables.

The simple language structures of this text are supported by high-quality images that support reading for information. Whilst there is repetition of a small number of useful high frequency words, they are used in a several simple language structures. This means that the child has to pay focused attention to the print to use known letters and words.

Learning outcomes

Children can:

- read known high frequency words in context quickly and fluently

- read a range of simple sentences independently across two lines of text and across a two page-spread

- use simple non-fiction features, such as tables, to support comprehension.

Developing reading comprehension

- Simple non-chronological report incorporates early features of non-fiction texts which explores the five senses.

- Includes common experiences with which young children will be familiar.

- Although there is no contents page, the first two pages provide an overall introduction to the text. Thought bubbles are introduced. A simple table (pages 14 and 15) provides additional information in graphic form.

Grammar and sentence structure

- Short clear sentences that follow natural language patterns.

- Three repetitive sentence structures, strongly supported by the illustrations and the placement of changing topic content on each page.

- Present tense used throughout as appropriate to report genre.

Word meaning and spelling

- Subject-specific vocabulary ('*taste/tasting*', '*smell/smelling*') is introduced, supported by the illustrations.

- Opportunity to read and rehearse known high frequency words ('*with*', '*Here*', '*my*') supported by the repeated sentences throughout the text.

- Exploring the inflectional ending /ing/ and noting the change of spelling for the root verb as in '*taste*' and '*tasting*'.

Curriculum links

Science and Nature – There are endless science experiments that can arise for a topic on the senses. Here are a few: Children can design feely boxes filled with different materials for their friends to identify; tasting or smelling to identify hidden items; listening for sounds in the environment or identifying musical instruments whilst blindfolded.

Maths – The science experiments above would lead to the generation of bar charts: children's favourite tastes or their worst smells, for example.

Title: In the Sea
Author: Claire Llewellyn

Genre: Non-fiction
Word count: 67

Overview

This simple non-fiction report gives information about the animals who make their home in the sea. The photographs provide enough detail to discuss how each animal moves and why it needs to make its home in the sea.

Learning outcomes

Children can:

- locate and read and write high-frequency words

- start to read in a more phrased manner while maintaining track of the print

- read simple words by sounding out and blending phonemes

- find information in non-fiction texts.

Developing reading comprehension

- Young readers may associate the word 'home' with a building. In this book, 'home' is used a little differently, to convey that the sea provides the habitat for each of the creatures in this book.

- The text provides opportunities to use the same vocabulary but used in different sequences, thus requiring the child to use visual information carefully.

Grammar and sentence structure

- Three lines of text on a page support consolidation of return sweep.

- Simple sentences using the indefinite article.

Word meaning and spelling

- Opportunity to rehearse and recognise frequently occurring words in context – 'This', 'is', 'in', 'the', 'A'.

- Words beginning with the same letter give the opportunity to look closely at print detail and cross check with the picture to check oral predictions ('seal', 'shrimp', 'shark').

Curriculum links

Science and Nature – This book would support a discussion of habitats. Animals make their homes in places that provide a food source and shelter. What do each of these animals need from their habitat?

Mathematics – Using the book, simple tables could be made to present information about whether each animal can breathe, whether they have scales, whether they come to the surface for example.

Title: The Weather Today
Author: Claire Llewellyn

Genre: Non-fiction
Word count: 102

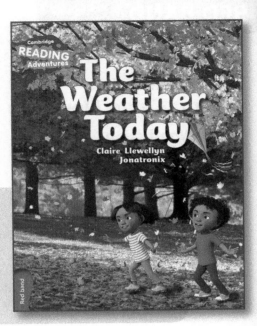

Overview

This book uses the weather reporter as a device to present the weather each day. The children then decide where to play. This provides a repetitive language structure that is useful to develop phrasing, fluency and expression with children reading at Red band.

Learning outcomes

Children can:

- read simple words by sounding out and blending phonemes left to right, including some two-syllable words comprising known chunks
- read a range of simple sentences independently, noting use of punctuation to pose questions
- find information in non-fiction texts.

Developing reading comprehension

- Simple information book using some non-fiction devices such as labels, headings and graphics to present the different weather conditions.
- The weather forecast itself on each two-page spread is given in the form of a speech bubble. The children in the book decide where they can play that day.

Grammar and sentence structure

- Repetitive sentence structures provide reading challenge by presenting a changing weather condition.
- Question and answer format.
- Prepositional language 'on the beach', 'in the park' is used as the children consider where they can play.

Word meaning and spelling

- Appropriate, subject-specific vocabulary ('rainy', 'snowy') is introduced, strongly supported by the illustrations.
- Regular high frequency words ('play', 'like') are reinforced by the repetitive structure.
- Some two-syllable words ('inside', 'today') which can be broken into known chunks for reading.

Curriculum links

Science and Nature – Children can create weather charts to track the weather over a period of time, devising their own weather symbols.

Drama – Watch weather forecasts on television or on the internet. Provide children with a large map of your country and have them roleplay giving the weather forecast for that day.

Title: Houses and Homes
Author: Lynne Rickards

Genre: Non-fiction
Word count: 96

Overview

This simple information book introduces early non-fiction features such as a simple index and the use of labelling. On each page, a different type of home is presented. The child living at each home indicates how they access their home.

Learning outcomes

Children can:

- read simple words by sounding out and blending phonemes left to right

- use syntax and context when reading for meaning

- locate and read and write high-frequency words

- find information in non-fiction texts.

Developing reading comprehension

- The reader encounters a range of homes from around the world which have very different entrances and exits.

- New vocabulary is introduced, supported by the illustrations and the opportunity to use visual discrimination within a strong sentence structure.

- Some of the names of the types of houses may be unfamiliar to the young reader.

Grammar and sentence structure

- Two lines of text on a page, with reading challenge in the second line as each different way of entering the house is explained.

- Simple sentences strongly supported by meaning.

Word meaning and spelling

- Opportunity to rehearse and use sounding out and blending to read unfamiliar words and new vocabulary ('lift', 'ramp')

- Regular high-frequency words reinforced and revisited through repeated language structures ('go', 'up', 'live', 'in').

Curriculum links

Geography - The book provides opportunity to explore both the familiar and unfamiliar types of homes around the world. Further exploration could be to look at building materials, or reasons why certain houses are built as they are (e.g. houses built on stilts in areas of potential flooding).

Art and Design – Children could design their own houses with unusual entrances and exits, and think about how these are adapted for the needs of the people living in them (such as ramps for wheelchair users).

Title: Imani's Library Book
Author: Alison Hawes

Genre: Fiction
Word count: 74

Overview

Children will recognize and identify with the situation in this story. Imani loves the book about dinosaurs. When it is time to take it back to the library, Imani cannot find another book he likes as much as the dinosaur one, so he ends up taking the same book home again.

Learning outcomes

Children can:

- use punctuation to inform phrasing and expression
- use phonic knowledge to solve new and novel words
- comment on the events and characters in the story, making links to other stories.

Developing reading comprehension

- A strong match between illustrations and the texts supports the reading of unfamiliar words and maintaining meaning.
- Opportunity to discuss rationales (explaining why Imani might like the dinosaur book so much).

Grammar and sentence structure

- One long sentence consolidates one-to-one correspondence and return sweep. The goal at this band is for the children to follow the print with their eyes, only rarely using finger-pointing at points of difficulty.
- Punctuation (full stop, elision and exclamation marks) supports phrased and expressive reading.

Word meaning and spelling

- Opportunity to rehearse and read a wide range of known high frequency words.
- Practice and consolidation of reading regular decodable words.

Curriculum links

Maths – Information about how many books the children have read and on what topics could be gathered over a week in school and presented in tally charts and graphs.

Language development – Discuss why Imani is so keen on the book about dinosaurs. Then create a short time slot each day where children can recommend what they have read to other children. Ask them to talk about why they enjoyed it and why it might be a good book for other children to read.

Title: What Little Kitten Wants
Author: Kathryn Harper

Genre: Fiction
Word count: 101

Overview

Min and Lee have a new baby kitten. Min thinks that Little Kitten wants to play with her like a toy. Poor Little Kitten. Big brother Lee helps Min to understand that Little Kitten needs to be treated gently. With the help of his book about kittens, Min and Lee learn how to care for Little Kitten.

Learning outcomes

Children can:

- use punctuation to inform phrasing and expression
- use phonic knowledge to solve new and novel words
- comment on the events and characters in the story, making links to other stories and non-fiction texts.

Developing reading comprehension

- The relationship between brother and sister can be explored through actions and intentions, such as Lee's finding a book to help Min understand how to care for kittens.
- Development of inference is supported – why does Min want a kitten?

Grammar and sentence structure

- Consistency of text presentation and some repetition of sentence patterns supports the reader to match one-to-one across two to three lines of text on each page.
- Punctuation (full stop, question mark and exclamation mark) supports phrased and expressive reading.
- Use of a simple contraction 'doesn't'.

Word meaning and spelling

- Opportunity to rehearse and recognise frequently occurring words in context – 'said', 'to', 'want', 'Stop',
- Sound out simple words and blend phonemes from left to right.

Curriculum links

Science - Animals need to be looked after properly. They must be treated well whether kept as pets or as part of farming. Choose a range of animals kept in the locality and make a chart of the things that they need. The chart might have headings of *Food, Housing, Exercise, Care.*

PSHE – Develop posters showing how to look after a kitten. The children could illustrate ways of playing with, feeding, exercising and playing with a kitten.

Title: A House for Snail
Author: Vivian French

Genre: Fiction
Word count: 187

Overview

Snail wants a house. He travels from creature to creature asking if he can live with them. Snail is unsuited to each of the homes – too heavy, too big, unable to wriggle under the ground or fly. Then one of the animals points out to Snail that he is carrying a house on his back – one that it is ideally suited to his needs.

Learning outcomes

Children can:

- use punctuation to inform phrasing and expression
- use phonic knowledge to solve new and novel words
- comment on the events and characters in the story, making links to other stories.

Developing reading comprehension

- Snail looks for a house, only to find that he has been carrying the ideal home on his back all the time. The question-answer structure of the book is a good opportunity to use reading expression. How is Snail feeling at each subsequent rejection?
- Snail's search is told through a repetitive structure with lots of opportunities for developing reading with phrasing as the characters interact. This learning objective is best supported by encouraging children to follow the print with their eyes, only rarely using finger-pointing at points of difficulty.

Grammar and sentence structure

- Some repetition of phrase patterns, but with more variation of sentence structure evident.
- Fully punctuated question and answer structure.
- Familiar oral language structures with some literary language.

Word meaning and spelling

- Opportunity to rehearse a wide range of known high frequency words.
- Practice and consolidation of reading regular decodable words.

Curriculum links

Science and Nature – Animals make their homes in many different places. In this book, Snail finds out that he is not suited to a home in a web, in a hive or under the ground. This book links to finding out about animal habitats.

Title: Diego Fandango
Author: Lynne Rickards

Genre: Fiction
Word count: 155

Overview

Diego Fandango wants to play in a band. He gathers some friends together and they organise a concert. Just as they are about to begin, it starts to rain and their audience runs for cover. Oh no! Diego and his friends may not be able to play. But then the rain stops. A rainbow provides the perfect backdrop for such a colourful concert.

Learning outcomes

Children can:

• read aloud using the context, sentence structure and sight vocabulary to read with expression and for meaning

• attempt new words in more challenging texts using their phonic knowledge

• comment on the events and characters in the story, making imaginative links to their own experience.

Developing reading comprehension

• In this humorous and colourfully illustrated text, Diego the Flamingo wants to play in a band, and looks for fellow musicians to play with him. A problem and resolution work to provide a simple story structure and time sequence.

Grammar and sentence structure

• Some repetition of phrase patterns, but with more variation of sentence structure evident.

• Punctuation, including the use of exclamation marks and speech marks, supports phrased and fluent reading.

• Familiar oral language structures combined with some literary language.

Word meaning and spelling

• Opportunity to rehearse a wide range of known high frequency words.

• Practice and consolidation of reading regular decodable words.

• Use of 'shouted' and 'said' to report speech.

Curriculum links

Music – Each animal played a different instrument. Listen to a piece of music to identify each instrument. What instrument is playing? Compare different instruments.

Religious studies – Linked to festivals and celebrations: why might people put on a show?

Title: Late for School
Author: Claire Llewellyn

Genre: Fiction
Word count: 184

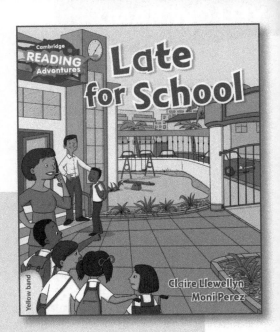

Overview

In this story from the International School strand, Omar and his friends all fear they will be late for school. Luckily, they are able to overcome the challenges by arriving at school on time. But, when they get to school, they find that it is Miss Garcia that is late. Her bike got a punctured tyre as she swerved to avoid a cat in the road. She arrives at school, very dishevelled.

The rise in challenge involves a variety of language structures to express the story and inferences contained in both picture and text as to why the children and Miss Garcia are late. The repetition of key phrases (*'We are going to be late for school.'*, for example) provide good opportunities for building fluency.

Learning outcomes

Children can:

- read more challenging texts using phonic word recognition and knowledge of known high frequency words

- pay attention to syntax and punctuation to aid reading for meaning

- comment on the events in the story, making links with what is known already about the characters, and children's own experience.

Developing reading comprehension

- This is a book in the International School strand of *Cambridge Reading Adventures* which features Omar and his friends. Children may have read other books in this series and will know the character traits. In this story, all the characters are worried about being late for school. The twist in the tale is that they all arrive at school before their teacher!

- Inference is required to gain precise meaning behind the reasons that the characters are late. Some are genuinely worried (*'Oh No!' says Leila.'*), whilst others are the cause of the situation (*'Omar stops to look at the fish in the pond.'*).

Grammar and sentence structure

- Repetition of phrase patterns, although some variation of structure as events build.

- Oral reading is supported by speech punctuation and exclamations.

- Use of present tense throughout to build tension.

Word meaning and spelling

- Known high frequency words are used in familiar phrases and natural language.

- Opportunity for practice in reading regular decodable words.

- Some unfamiliar vocabulary (*'tuk-tuk'*) and uses of word tense (*'does'*) that require attention to letter detail.

Curriculum links

Social Studies – Children can map their journeys to school and chart the different modes of transport used. The topic could also extend to modes of transport around the world, and link with history topics on transport.

Maths – Make graphs and charts of the different ways children in the class travel to school. How long does each journey take?

Title: Oh Bella!
Author: Lauri Kubuitsile

Genre: Fiction
Word count: 165

Overview

Bella likes to help her family. But it doesn't always go to plan. She carries some water for Mum, but spills it. She tries to hang washing out, but ends up making Papa's task harder. She tries to help Hugo but ends up falling into the river. It isn't long before no one wants Bella to help. Bella is sad. But then Tessa comes up with the perfect opportunity to help. She asks Bella to help in the garden. Bella helps plant the seeds. Every day, she waters the plants. It isn't long before they have a watermelon to share with the family. Bella's help has worked. She is a good helper.

Learning outcomes

Children can:

- read more challenging texts using phonic knowledge along with automatic recognition of high-frequency words
- take more note of punctuation to support the use of grammar and oral language rhythms
- comment on events, characters, and ideas, making imaginative links to their own experience.

Developing reading comprehension

- Bella really wants to help but her efforts cause more trouble. Building over a series of events, Bella finally finds something she can do to help.

- Some of the events in the story are informed by the pictures rather than explicitly described in the text. The reader has to think about what they already know of Bella to understand why she ends up hanging on the washing line and falling into the river.

- Further inference is needed to understand why growing things might be a good thing for Bella to help with.

Grammar and sentence structure

- Some repetition to support reading for expression. Sentence structures change as the story builds, encouraging careful attention to print detail.

- Punctuation aids expression and reading for meaning.

Word meaning and spelling

- Opportunity to rehearse regular phonically decodable words ('*let*', '*help*', '*drop*').

- Introduction of the word 'asked' supported in context of the repeated question '*Can I help you?*'

- Spelling of verbs using the inflection 'ing' (such as '*hanging*', '*helping*')

Curriculum links

PSHE – linked with people who help us. Also, to explore family relationships and support. Why didn't her family want Bella to help?

Science and Nature – linking to a project on things that grow. Bella waters her plant every day – what would happen if she forgot to water it? Or over-watered it?

Title: Little Tiger Hu can Roar!
(Benchmark Text)
Author: Gabby Pritchard

Genre: Fiction
Word count: 177

Overview

Little Tiger Hu has recently learned how to roar. He creeps up behind Elephant, Hippo and Monkey as they are feeding. He enjoys scaring them, and watches in delight as they run away in terror. But then he creeps up on Hare and tries to scare him. Hare is not scared. Hare knows that Little Tiger Hu is a baby. Little Tiger Hu has found a friend. They run off together to play.

Learning outcomes

Children can:

- read more challenging texts using phonic knowledge along with automatic recognition of high-frequency words

- use syntax and context when reading for meaning

- interpret a text by reading aloud with some variety of pace and emphasis

- comment on events, characters, and ideas, making imaginative links to their own experience.

Developing reading comprehension

- This humorous story follows a pattern seen in many traditional tales where a sequence is built up over several episodes. It uses some simple literary language which may need to be supported.

- At Yellow band, the reader has to make some deductions about the characters in the story to get the full meaning. Here, Little Tiger Hu is a baby trying out a new skill and that inference is an important element in understanding why Hare is not scared.

Grammar and sentence structure

- The position of the adverb at the beginning of the sentence for dramatic effect - *'Slowly, slowly he went ...'*

- Complex sentence - *'even if they have a big roar.'* (page 12)

Word meaning and spelling

- Check knowledge of prepositions *'over'*, *'into'*, *'through'*.

- Reinforce 'ee' words in context *'three'*, *'tree'*, *'see'*, *'green'*.

Curriculum links

Geography – Little Tiger Hu creeps up on the animals by moving around the forest and the field. This context could be used to develop geography activities, mapping landscape features and creating routes around different landscapes.

Music – Listening activities using different environmental sounds could build on the idea of listening carefully to the sounds around you.

YELLOW BAND

Title: My School
Author: Shoua Fakhouri

Genre: Non-fiction
Word count: 253

Overview

The children arrive at school ready to start their day. We are shown where they line up to go into school, how they start their day, which lessons they have, what they do at playtime and how their teachers help them, using the structure of the school day as the presentation sequence.

Learning outcomes

Children can:

- read aloud using the context, sentence structure and sight vocabulary to read with expression and for meaning
- attempt new words in more challenging texts using phonic knowledge
- comment on the information in the text making links to their own experience.

Developing reading comprehension

- This chronological recount is written in the continuous present tense, which is not typical for the genre. The personal voice 'we' is used throughout.
- A typical day in school forms the structure of the book. Page headings and a contents page support the thematic presentation.
- Good control of print location and early reading behaviours are required as text is presented on both the left hand and right hand pages, with some pages having up to five lines of text.

Grammar and sentence structure

- Use of vocabulary of comparative time commonly used in reporting genres ('The first lesson', The next lesson', Then', 'Today').
- Punctuation and line placement support the development of phrased reading.
- Personal voice structures typical of recounts ('We can', 'We go', 'We like').

Word meaning and spelling

- Opportunity to rehearse a wide range of known high frequency words ('to,' 'in', 'the', 'we', 'is', 'and').
- Consolidate reading regular decodable words.
- Opportunity to use print detail to read two-syllable words formed from two words ('outside', 'Everyone', 'inside', 'playground').

Curriculum links

Science and Nature – In this school, sometimes it is too hot to play outside and the children have to play with their friends inside. Children could suggest ways of making sure that children keep cool at playtimes and that playgrounds have enough shade, possibly linking with another Yellow band text in *Cambridge Reading Adventures*, 'Playgrounds'.

Maths – What happens in your school day? Sequence the school day using times to develop the use of sequencing language and rehearse telling the time.

Title: Playgrounds
Author: Lynne Rickards

Genre: Non-fiction
Word count: 102

Overview

The text reports on a variety of types of playgrounds, including those in unusual places and those that look a little different. The context of a playground is likely to be familiar to children, but the range of different types will not be.

The language structures use a range of high frequency words, but in different places within the sentences. This demands consistent use of print information in order to monitor accuracy of reading and makes for a good learning opportunity to consolidate high frequency word knowledge.

The text draws the reader in and, in keeping with Yellow band, provides the reader with the opportunity to comment on the relationship between the context of the illustrations and their own experiences and preferences.

Learning outcomes

Children can:

- read aloud using the context, sentence structure and sight vocabulary to read with expression and for meaning

- attempt new words in more challenging texts using phonic knowledge

- comment on the information in the text, making links to their own experience.

Developing reading comprehension

- This non-chronological report explores some important features of playgrounds; how they look, where they are and what children can do.

- The reader is required to have control of print location and one-to-one correspondence as the text appears at both the top and bottom of the page, with some sentences going on to two lines of text.

- 'Safe' has particular connotations in this text; it would be useful to discuss what it means to be safe when playing in a playground and how playgrounds are designed to keep children safe.

Grammar and sentence structure

- Some repetition of phrase patterns commonly used in reporting genres ('Some playgrounds are'; 'This playground is').

- Punctuation and line placement support the development of phrased reading.

- Sentence structures typical of non-fiction reports ('Children can') with some use of familiar oral language ('It's fun').

Word meaning and spelling

- Opportunity to rehearse a wide range of known high frequency words ('can', 'look', 'like', 'made').

- Practice and consolidation of reading regular decodable words.

- Opportunity to use print detail to read for the precise meaning ('in', inside').

Curriculum links

Language Development – Speaking and Listening activities could develop the use of simile. In the book, 'This slide looks like a red snake'. Photographs or pictures on iPads could be used for discussion, for example, 'This path looks like (a winding snake, a wiggly worm).', 'The moon looks like... (a shining light, a yellow mirror, a piece of cheese)'.

Mathematics – The playgrounds have slides, tunnels and turrets. The pictures could be used to reinforce the naming vocabulary of three dimensional solid shapes – cylinder, cuboid, sphere, cube, triangular prism.

Title: Stars
Author: Lauri Kubuitsile

Genre: Non-fiction
Word count: 135

Overview

What are stars? What are they made of? Are they close to the earth? On each page, an astronomer presents interesting facts about stars, taking us through general information and specific types of stars.

Learning outcomes

Children can:

- track the print with their eyes, finger-pointing only at points of difficulty
- search for information in print to attempt and confirm new words while reading
- make links between this text and other non-fiction texts they have read.

Developing reading comprehension

- This non-chronological report uses the device of an 'expert' scientist to provide information and this serves as a guide through the book for the reader.
- Simple non-fiction features such as headings, captions and diagrams are included.
- A glossary supports comprehension of subject-specific vocabulary.

Grammar and sentence structure

- Verb usage is typical of non-fiction reports: '*Stars are …*'. '*The sun is …*'
- Some simple use of causal connectives: '*It looks big because it is close to the earth.*'
- More variation of sentence structure.

Word meaning and spelling

- The text includes a wide range of known high frequency words ('*is*', '*are*', '*the*', '*in*') which children can read automatically to support phrased, fluent reading.
- Compound words ('*supergiants*', '*outside*', '*cannot*') which can be broken into chunks for reading.
- New, unfamiliar words ('*dust*', '*gas*') can be decoded using phonic knowledge, with contextual meaning gained through the use of the glossary.

Curriculum links

Science and Nature – This text will support non-fiction topics on space and space travel. Children could also explore the use of simple telescopes. Exploring perspective (that objects look smaller when they are further away) could be an interesting activity.

Drama – The book is narrated by a scientific 'expert'. As part of a non-fiction topic children could assume the role of expert to explain what they have found out about stars. This could form a short video presentation.

Title: Help!
Author: Gabby Pritchard

Genre: Fiction
Word count: 128

Overview

Lizard likes eating bugs and insects. He eats too much and gets stuck in a crevice between two rocks. Luckily a little ladybird is able to soothe him to sleep and when Lizard wakes in the morning, his stomach has shrunk sufficiently to escape from the rocks. But will he eat the ladybird?

Learning outcomes

Children can:

- read aloud using the context, sentence structure and sight vocabulary to read with expression and for meaning
- attempt new words in more challenging texts using their phonic knowledge
- comment on the events and characters in the story, making imaginative links to their own experience.

Developing reading comprehension

- This colourfully illustrated story has a problem and resolution structure, enabling the young reader to begin to discuss consequence of action and to predict outcome.
- Text appears on both pages and varies in its position on the page to support the story events, requiring well established direction and accurate one-to-one matching at this band.

Grammar and sentence structure

- some repetition of phrase patterns, but greater variation of sentence structure then in Red band
- Punctuation, including the use of exclamation marks and speech marks, supports phrased and fluent reading
- familiar oral language structures

Word meaning and spelling

- opportunity to rehearse a wide range of known high frequency words
- practice and consolidation of reading regular decodable words
- use of inflections 'ing' and 'ed'

Curriculum links

Music – The ladybird sang Lizard to sleep. Learn some lullabies in common use and talk about how the sounds, the type of melody and the words soother the listener to sleep.

Science and nature – Use non-fiction books and websites to explore the creatures that Lizards like to eat. This work could be displayed with captions created by the children.

Title: The Boy Who Said No
Author: Alex Eeles

Genre: Fiction
Word count: 128

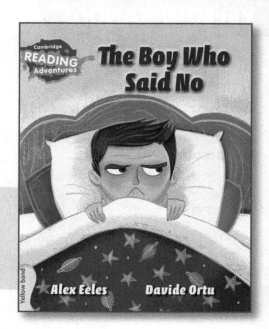

Overview

Zak is having a bad day. He doesn't want to get up and can't be persuaded. But seeing his family enjoying themselves brings him out of his mood and he joins them to play together.

Learning outcomes

Children can:

- read aloud using the context, sentence structure and sight vocabulary to read with expression and for meaning
- attempt new words in more challenging texts using their phonic knowledge
- comment on the events and characters in the story, making links to their own experience.

Developing reading comprehension

- The story deals with a context that will be familiar to children.
- Simple inferences are required to gain precise meaning of the text.

Grammar and sentence structure

- Some repetition of phrase patterns for effect and emphasis
- Punctuation, including the use of exclamation marks and speech marks, supports phrased and fluent reading
- Direct speech uses oral language structures

Word meaning and spelling

- opportunity to rehearse syllabifying with words that have two familiar words; out/side, up/stairs
- simple contraction 'didn't'
- Use of inflection 'ed'

Curriculum links

PSHE – Discuss with the children things that make them angry or frustrated. How do they manage those feelings? What can help cheer them up?

Maths – plan a decision-tree, with questions which can only be answered either yes or no, designed to find the hidden number. For example, can it be divided by 3? Is it an odd number?

Title: The Big City
Author: Lynne Rickards

Genre: Non-fiction
Word count: 98

Overview

In this simple first person recount, a young boy takes the reader through his day as we explore with him the sights and sounds of a big city.

Learning outcomes

Children can:

- orally syllabify words read in context to identify the phonemic chunks
- attempt new words in more challenging texts using phonic knowledge
- comment on the information in the text making links to their own experience.

Developing reading comprehension

- For some children, who may not have experienced life in a big city, the content and context may be challenging. Teachers will be making links with children's real-life experiences.
- Opportunity to compare and contrast the different ways in which humans live around the world.

Grammar and sentence structure

- Simple present tense sentence structures are used throughout.
- Punctuation and line placement support the development of phrased reading.
- Personal voice structures typical of recounts (*'I live 'I can', 'We go', 'We live'*).

Word meaning and spelling

- Opportunity to rehearse a wide range of known high frequency words (*can, see, of, are*).
- Consolidate reading regular decodable words.
- Opportunities to rehearse orally segmenting multisyllabic words (*'traffic', 'buildings', 'supermarket', 'beautiful'*).

Curriculum links

Geography – This book recounts a journey to the park via the supermarket. Do the children have a favourite place to spend their free time? Ask them to create a route map to this place, showing the amenities and landmarks that they pass.

PSHE – The boy has to be careful as he crosses the busy street. Discuss road safety with the children. Posters showing ways to stay safe as you cross the road could follow up this discussion.

Title: Where Are My Shoes?
Author: Sue Bodman and Glen Franklin

Genre: Fiction
Word count: 150

Overview

Taj is untidy. Everywhere Taj and mum go, he makes a mess and then can't find his shoes easily when it's time to go home. He gets his come-uppance at a children's party when he has to go home with just one shoe.

Learning outcomes

Children can:

- read aloud using the context, sentence structure and sight vocabulary to read with expression and for meaning

- attempt new words in more challenging texts using their phonic knowledge

- comment on the events and characters in the story, making links to their own experience.

Developing reading comprehension

- The story uses familiar settings and events to ensure that the inferences required to gain precise meaning of the text are simple and straightforward.

- Children will need to make the connection between Taj's untidiness and his missing shoe in the last sequence, thinking about what Taj could have done to avoid this outcome.

Grammar and sentence structure

- Longer sentences (e.g. *'He took off his shoes and went into the water.'* p.3) are supported by shorter sentences (e.g. *'Look at this mess!'* p.3) so that the increase in challenge is measured and supportive.

- Punctuation, including the use of exclamation marks and speech marks, supports phrased and fluent reading.

- Direct speech uses natural language structures.

Word meaning and spelling

- Natural language structures *'Here they are'*, *'Look at this mess'*.

- Familiar phonemes can be blended to check context words (e.g. *sand, pool, mess*).

- Use of inflection 'ed'

Curriculum links

PSHE – Discuss with the children the ways that they can take responsibility for themselves and their belongings, as appropriate to their age. This could be the basis of a classroom responsibility system and rota.

Mathematics – Taj should have a pair of shoes. Explore the term 'pairs' in different contexts. Younger children could find identical pairs amongst objects or picture cards. Slightly older children could find functional pairs (i.e. hammer and nail) or related pairs (i.e. sheep and a jumper) or calculate pairs of numbers for the same total.

Title: Lost!
Author: Gaby Pritchard

Genre: Fiction
Word count: 206

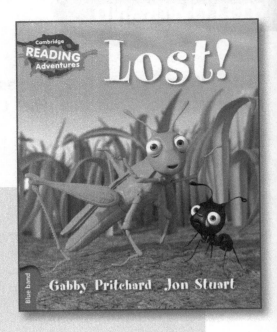

Overview

A cricket takes a nap. He is awoken by the sound of crying. A little ant has lost his family. The cricket resolves to help and they set off to look for the ant's family. After leaping from place to place, they eventually spot the ant's nest and family members when they jump up into a tree. The cricket returns to his nap, pleased to have helped.

The text requires the reader to interpret the text and make some causal connections ('the talking leaf' which represents the little ant). The speech between characters is helpful to continue to build reading with expression. The text contains hints to interpret the characters more fully than at previous bands.

Learning outcomes

Children can:

- read aloud with appropriate pace and emphasis, noting punctuation
- attend to print, meaning, and sentence structure flexibly to support automatic self-correction
- decode phonically regular words fast so that fluency of reading is maintained.

Developing reading comprehension

- In a story about helping, a tiny ant is lost and a cricket helps him to find his way home. A sequence of events occurs. Causal connections aid comprehension throughout the storyline, whilst pictures offer support without conveying the precise meaning (page 11, for example).

Grammar and sentence structure

- Longer sentences, including use of conjunctions ('*They jumped from nest to nest but they did not find the ant's home.*') and adjectival phrases ('*over the long grass*', '*under the leaf*').
- Dialogue is fully punctuated with question marks and exclamation marks used to support expressive reading and to emphasise character ('*Can I help you, little ant?*', '*That's my brother!*').
- Use of elision ('*I'm*', '*Let's*') mirrors natural speech patterns.

Word meaning and spelling

- Alternative spellings of the digraph /ee/ ('*tree*', '*leaf*' '*me*').
- Spelling of regular past tense verbs ('*jumped*', '*opened*') with /ed/ inflectional endings.

Curriculum links

Science and Nature – The story could provide a fictional backdrop for a study of mini-beasts. Research habitats of ants, using non-fiction texts and the internet.

PSHE – The cricket is a natural predator of ants, yet in this story he helps the ant find his way home. Read stories where people have helped others, such as the biblical story of the Good Samaritan.

Title: Suli's Big Race
Author: Alex Eeles

Genre: Fiction
Word count: 215

Overview

Suli the elephant likes running, but she is not very fast. She accepts a challenge to race Taz the cheetah. All the other animals are convinced that Taz will win. The race begins and Taz takes an early lead. Suli keeps going and refuses to give up. Then Taz is distracted; he looks back to see how far behind Suli is. He doesn't see a muddy puddle and falls headlong into it. Suli wins the race.

'*Slowcoach*' is repeated several times in the story, in two different language structures ('*Slowcoach Suli*'; '*a slowcoach again.*') presenting multiple opportunities to use phonic skills to check word detail.

Learning outcomes

Children can:

- read aloud demonstrating appropriate pace and emphasis

- comment on events and characters, using the text to support their opinions

- decode single syllable words using their phonic knowledge, with fast visual recall of known high frequency words.

Developing reading comprehension

- This story is an innovation on the fable of the Tortoise and the Hare. Children will be able to make links with their own experiences and with other stories in which the underdog triumphs in the end. Suli is not an object of ridicule but an example of how strong character and tenacity are admirable personal qualities. See also 'The Lion and The Mouse' (Green band) for another retelling of a traditional fable.

- The reader needs to understand that Suli is to be admired for maintaining her resolve. The clues to that are in the word choice, rather than stated explicitly and represent a challenge to reading comprehension skills that is encountered at Blue band.

Grammar and sentence structure

- Some use of literary language ('*One day*') and repeated phrases ('*I must keep going!*').

- Speech punctuation serves to track continued dialogue after the reporting clause, such as on page 14.

- Both regular past tense verbs with /ed/ inflections and irregular past tense verbs ('*ran*', '*came*') are featured.

Word meaning and spelling

- Adjectives describe appearance and add to character description ('*long grass*', '*little legs*', '*big rocks*').

- The level of challenge provides opportunity for children to decode single syllable CVC words fluently using their growing phonic knowledge.

Curriculum links

Physical Education – Children will be familiar with races and school sports. Set up an obstacle course for a class race (but perhaps not with mud!).

PSHE – Running is one way of keeping fit. The text would support work on health, well-being and exercise.

Title: A Day at the Museum
Author: Sibel Sagner

Genre: Fiction
Word count: 254

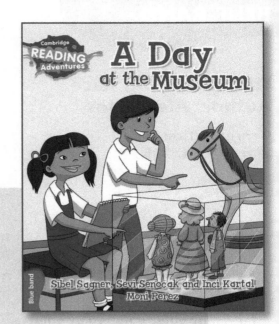

Overview

Miss Garcia's class visit a museum. Each of the children draw one of the exhibits. Zara draws one of the dolls, Omar draws a detailed picture of a horse skeleton. Zara asks Miss Garcia if they can make a museum at school. Miss Garcia thinks that this is a wonderful idea and when they get back to school, the children set about making some exhibits. Omar begins to wish that he had drawn something else, as now he has to find something to use to make all the bones of a horse's skeleton. That's going to be a tricky job!

Learning outcomes

Children can:

- solve unfamiliar words using print information and understanding of the text

- sustain accurate reading over a greater number of lines of text on a page

- comment on events, characters, and ideas, making imaginative links to their own experience.

Developing reading comprehension

- This is a book in the International School strand of *Cambridge Reading Adventures* featuring Omar and his friends. In this story, the children visit a museum, and Zara has a good idea. But Omar has a problem to solve at the end. The story has a sequence of events, occurring over time and in different venues.

- Pictures support the storyline rather than illustrating the exact meaning, requiring more inferential reading.

Grammar and sentence structure

- Sentence patterns and structures are more varied.

- Speech is sustained over more than one sentence.

Word meaning and spelling

- Fast automatic recognition of high frequency words.

- Decoding new and unfamiliar words, supported by context and meaning.

Curriculum links

Science and Nature – Study of animal bones and skeletons. Linked to work on fossils and dinosaur bones.

History – Beno says the doll looks older than his grandpa. Children could ask grandparents about toys they played with when they were young. How were they different to modern day toys?

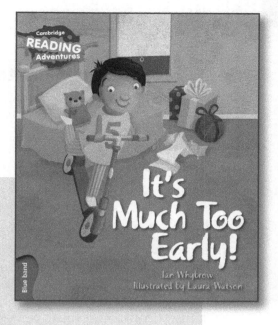

Title: It's Much Too Early!
Author: Ian Whybrow

Genre: Fiction
Word count: 269

Overview

Jamal wakes up on his birthday. He opens his presents. He receives a scooter and wants to ride it immediately. But it's only five o'clock. Mum and Dad and his brother all encourage him to go back to bed. But Jamal gets up, opens his scooter and proceeds to race around the house. At seven o'clock, he is persuaded to go back to bed. But at eight o'clock, when the rest of the family want to get and celebrate Jamal's birthday, he is back in bed, protesting that it is much too early.

The structure of the story through the use of time provide clues to reading comprehension. The refrain '*It's much too early!*' provides some useful repetition to build reading fluency.

Learning outcomes

Children can:

- monitor their own errors and show a greater degree of self-correction

- reread to check meaning is conveyed through phrasing and expression

- discuss the story to demonstrate understanding.

Developing reading comprehension

- The story follows a sequence of events with a twist at the end, when Jamal himself thinks it's much too early to get up! Illustrations are used to supplement information provided in the text and to provide inferential links.

- A greater number of lines on the page (between five and seven) help to develop reading stamina for longer texts. In turn, story meaning is developed over a greater number of pages. This text is a fully developed story and requires discussion to establish understanding.

Grammar and sentence structure

- Repeated language patterns act as refrains, including the title: '*It's Much Too Early!*'

- Speech punctuation indicates the different characters speaking, such as the conversation between Jamal and Dad on pages 4 and 5.

- Sentence lengths vary to create effect, for example using short sentences in dialogue: '*Here I come!*' on page 9.

Word meaning and spelling

- Two syllable words ('*birthday*', '*downstairs*') can be read by identifying known parts of words.

- Opportunity to rehearse automatic, fast recognition of high-frequency words.

Curriculum links

Maths – Use the story to think about what happens at different times of the day: What time do children get up? What time do they come to school? Make links with other books in *Cambridge Reading Adventures* that show the passage of time across a day, such as 'My School' (Yellow band).

Literacy – Jamal was really excited that he had a scooter for his birthday. Children could write about their favourite birthday present, or about something they would really like to receive on their next birthday.

Title: The Pumpkin Monster (Benchmark Text)
Author: Susan Gates

Genre: Fiction
Word count: 181

Overview

Hanna grows a pumpkin. But it grows far larger than she had anticipated. At first, everyone admires the pumpkin, but it grows into a monster. The Pumpkin Monster wants feeding and rolls away to look for things to eat, devouring the villagers' corn. As it seeks out yet more food, it rolls over a sharp thorn. The Pumpkin Monster meets its end, dwindling away until only a little orange puddle can be seen.

In this text, simple literary language such as *'was like a little orange puddle'* requires the reader to interpret the text and make connections.

Dialogue mixes oral language structures (*'Get rid of that pumpkin'*) and more literary structures (*'That's the biggest pumpkin we have ever seen'*).

Learning outcomes

Children can:

- comment on events and characters, using the text to support their opinions

- monitor their own errors and show a greater degree of self-correction

- demonstrate automatic recall of known high frequency words.

Developing reading comprehension

- This tale follows a familiar cumulative story framework, such as that used in 'The Gingerbread Man'. A pumpkin grows bigger and bigger until it becomes a monster, but Hanna saves the day and the pumpkin gets his comeuppance.

- Levels of inference are required, for example making the causal link between the sharp thorns and the deflated monster. It would be helpful to discuss these links and turns of phrase to ensure that the young readers understand the abstracted and literary language.

Grammar and sentence structure

- Sentences vary in length, for example, longer sentences separated by a reporting clause to build suspense: *'Stop eating our corn,' said Hanna, 'or we will be hungry.'* (page 10).

- Use of literary language (*'as big as a house'*) and repeated phrases (*'I want food!'*).

- Complex sentences including adverbial phrases, such as *'Hanna chased the pumpkin into a forest.'* (page 12).

Word meaning and spelling

- Use of onomatopoeia (*'Psssssst'* on page 13) to describe the pumpkin deflating.

- Comparative and superlative adjectives (*'big'*, *'bigger and bigger'*, *'biggest'*) are used to demonstrate the growth of the pumpkin.

Curriculum links

Science and Nature – Projects on growing, such as children planting their own pumpkin seeds. Whose pumpkin will grow the biggest?

History – Hanna is very brave. Use nonfiction books and the internet to look for true life stories of heroines in your context.

Title: My First Train Trip
Author: Lynne Rickards

Genre: Non-fiction
Word count: 236

Overview

A little girl and her mum go to visit Grandpa. Each stage of the journey is recounted: They depart from a busy train station; they have to find the correct platform; they find their seats on the train; as the train starts to move, they pass through first the city, then the countryside; finally they reach the place where Grandpa lives.

Learning outcomes

Children can:

- solve new words using print information and understanding of the text
- track accurately across six lines of text on a page.

Developing reading comprehension

- This text explains a child's journey by train to see Grandpa. Presented chronologically, we are taken through the process of setting out, buying a ticket, taking the journey and arriving at the destination.

Grammar and sentence structure

- Use of chronological vocabulary, such as 'Soon', 'Now' and 'At last'.
- Impersonal sentence structures integrated with direct speech to reflect the genre.

Word meaning and spelling

- Two syllable words to develop decoding skills (for example, 'platform', 'Grandpa', 'window').

Curriculum links

Speaking and Listening skills – Sequencing activities involving journeys. The context of this activity requires journeys with a clear order. Stories such as 'Rosie's Walk', 'Handa's Surprise' or 'The Gingerbread Man' could be used for this type of activity.

Geography – Mapping activities of a journey children take when they visit friends or family.

Title: Making a Car
Author: Claire Llewellyn

Genre: Non-fiction
Word count: 267

Overview

Cars are made in factories. The process of making a car has many stages; cutting the steel; making and painting the body; fitting the parts and the engine and a thorough final check. Each stage is explained and illustrated in the non-fiction report.

Learning outcomes

Children can:

- solve new words using print information and understanding of the text
- understand how a procedural text works.

Developing reading comprehension

- This non-fiction text takes us through the process of making a car. Technical terms are well-defined and the layout offers lots of opportunities to learn how to use simple non-fiction features such as a glossary and captions.

Grammar and sentence structure

- Use of chronological presentation and vocabulary, such as 'First', 'Next', 'Then' and 'Now'.
- Impersonal sentence structures in keeping with non-fiction genre.

Word meaning and spelling

- Two and three syllable words to develop decoding skills (for example, 'factory', 'assembly', 'machines', 'robots').

Curriculum links

Design Technology – Design cars; children could use junk modelling and construction toys to build their cars after designing.

Science and Nature – Children could explore materials (wood, metal, paper, plastic, etc.) for their various properties and qualities.

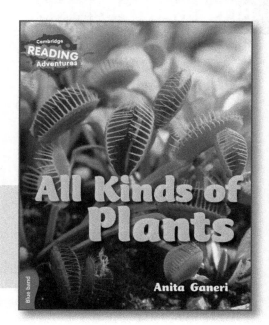

Title: All Kinds of Plants
Author: Anita Ganeri

Genre: Non-fiction
Word count: 188

Overview

Plants come in many different colours shapes and sizes. This book explains the main types of plants and looks at some interesting and unusual examples.

Learning outcomes

Children can:

- reread to clarify precise meaning after problem-solving of novel or less well-known words

- understand the features of non-chronological reports

- attend to changes in sentence structure, considering authorial impact.

Developing reading comprehension

- This non-chronological report explores different types of plants from all around the world. A range of non-fiction features support the text: labels and captions provide supplementary information, and the book includes a contents page, an index and a glossary.

- The book will provide a useful starting point for science work on growth and living things, and could link with 'Water' (Pink A band) and 'Where Do They Grow?' (Pink B band).

Grammar and sentence structure

- Grammatical features of non-chronological reports are used: continuous present tense, an impersonal sentence structure and a focus on generic participants.

- Captions are fully punctuated whilst labels are not.

- Sentence lengths are sometimes shorter to make the point more clearly: 'A fly lands on the leaves. The leaves snap shut.'

Word meaning and spelling

- Technical vocabulary and unfamiliar words are defined in the glossary.

- Two and three syllable words ('redwood', 'flytrap', 'rainforest') can be read in chunks, looking for known parts within the words.

Curriculum links

Science and Nature – Link to the plants that grow in your region: for example, children could visit a rice field or an orchard to study plants growing. Children can grow vegetables or fruit in the school garden. Plants that grow very tall very quickly (such as sunflowers) can be measured and planting conditions compared.

Literacy – Many stories use a plant or vegetable to innovate on a traditional tale (for example, 'The Pumpkin Monster' in Green band). Children could use a traditional tale such as 'The Enormous Turnip' as a framework to innovate on a story about one of the plants in this text: 'The Gigantic Cactus' for example.

Title: On the Track
Author: Claire Llewellyn

Genre: Non-fiction
Word count: 299

Overview

This book takes us through some different types of athletics events, providing clear definitions and a simple overview of how to do them. The reader can learn about sprinting, the hurdles, the long jump and high jump, and the javelin.

Learning outcomes

Children can:

- solve novel, unfamiliar words using print information, checking to ensure the meaning is understood
- understand the different features of report and procedure (instructional) writing
- comment on what they have read, relating to their own experience.

Developing reading comprehension

- A non-fiction text of mixed genre, this book explores the various athletics track and field events. The non-chronological report element describes each sport, whilst procedural features are used in the 'How to ...' sports guides sections.
- Technical terms are defined in the glossary. Photographs and diagrams demonstrate the various processes involved in each sport.

Grammar and sentence structure

- Sentences follow the grammatical conventions for each genre, such as continuous present tense for report writing, and the use of imperative verbs when giving instructions.
- Labels are unpunctuated, demonstrating the correct convention for this non-fiction feature.
- Adverbial phrases ('*towards the board*', '*into a pit of sand*') extend meaning in sentences.

Word meaning and spelling

- Unfamiliar, novel vocabulary is supported through the context and the glossary.
- Spelling of comparative and superlative adjectives ('*high*', '*higher*', '*highest*').

Curriculum links

Physical Education – children may not have experienced some of these athletic sports. Try some out during a PE lesson, ensuring the relevant safety measures are in place (and possibly omitting the javelin!)

History – children may be studying ancient cultures such as the Greeks or Romans. Many of these athletic sports come from ancient times. For example, children could read about the origins of the Olympic Games in Greece in non-fiction texts and on the internet.

Title: Crabs
Author: Ralph Hall

Genre: Non-fiction
Word count: 234

Overview

This simple non-chronological report focuses on crabs, exploring their distinct features, their different habitats and their eating habits.

Learning outcomes

Children can:

- re-read to clarify precise meaning after problem-solving of novel or less well-known words
- understand the features of non-chronological reports
- attend to changes in sentence structure, considering authorial impact.

Developing reading comprehension

- Labels and captions provide supplementary information, and the book includes a picture glossary.
- Words with specific topic usage are emboldened and defined in a glossary to support comprehension.

Grammar and sentence structure

- Grammatical features of non-chronological reports are used: continuous present tense, an impersonal sentence structure and a focus on generic participants.
- Captions are fully punctuated whilst labels are not.
- Sentence lengths are short to make the point more clearly: *'Crabs have ten legs.'* (p.4) *'Crabs eat plants. They eat animals, too.'* (p.6).

Word meaning and spelling

- Specific anatomic vocabulary is boldened and supported by a picture glossary.
- Two syllable words (*'outside'*, *'sideways'*, *'jellyfish'*) can be read in chunks, looking for known parts within the words.

Curriculum links

Science – Crustaceans do not all live in the sea. So why do such apparently different animals as crabs, lobsters, crayfish, shrimp, krill, woodlice and barnacles qualify as crustaceans? Discuss the key feature in common – the exoskeleton - and label some pictures with the three sections of their body – head, thorax, abdomen.

Art – Make models and images of crabs and other crustaceans using a variety of techniques – junk modelling with paper plates and bowls, hand prints and playdough, for example.

Title: The Show and Tell Day
Author: Sibel Sagner

Genre: Fiction
Word count: 227

Overview

This is a further book in the International School strand of the Cambridge Reading Adventure series. In this story, Miss Garcia holds a Show and Tell day, and the children share things about their home lives with their friends. As each child listens to the others, they build an empathy and understanding about their class mates.

Learning outcomes

Children can:

- solve unfamiliar words using print information and understanding of the text
- attend to the use of sentence structure and punctuation to support comprehension
- link their own experience to those of characters portrayed, explaining their reasons.

Developing reading comprehension

- Reading known high frequency words automatically and fluently to support comprehension.
- Prior knowledge of the characters and personal experience of a school setting enable the young reader to read with meaning and confidence.

Grammar and sentence structure

- Sentences are growing in complexity, including the use of fronted adverbial phrases (*'Here I am'* on p.5) and more complex constructions (such as embedding the reporting clause in speech on p.13).
- Speech punctuation is used to indicate different characters speaking (see, for example, p.11).

Word meaning and spelling

- Opportunity to rehearse automatic fast recognition of high-frequency or regular words
- Reading two-syllable words by identifying the known parts of words (*'everyone'*, *'display'*).

Curriculum links

Speaking and Listening – host a Show and Tell Day and ask children to talk about their object and why they have chosen it.

Literacy – Children can display their Show and Tell items and write captions to accompany them. Use non-fiction texts to follow the conventions for how captions are written

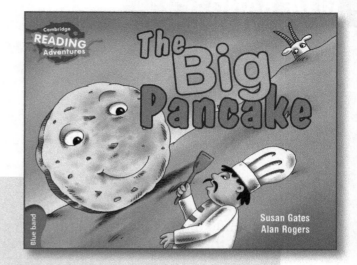

Title: The Big Pancake
Author: Susan Gates

Genre: Fiction
Word count: 245

Overview

In an innovative reworking of a traditional tale, a cook gives chase to the pancake he has made. Along the way, the pancake stops briefly to help a series of characters. They all give chase, too. The tale takes a change of direction as it becomes clear that they do not want to eat the pancake but say thank you for the help they have received.

Learning outcomes

Children can:

- solve unfamiliar words using print information and understanding of the text

- sustain accurate reading over a greater number of lines of text on a page

- comment on events, characters, and ideas, making imaginative links to their own experience

Developing reading comprehension

- The twist to the traditional retelling requires careful comprehension as the plot is not as might be expected.

- Cause and effect of motive and action can be explored in this simple tale.

Grammar and sentence structure

- Sentence patterns and structures are more varied.

- Speech is sustained over more than one utterance

- Longer sentences are created by adding characters to the repeated sequence.

Word meaning and spelling

- Use of comparatives *faster, biggest*

- decoding new and unfamiliar words, supported by context and meaning

- Opportunity to rehearse automatic, fast recognition of high-frequency words.

Curriculum links

Science – In this story, the pancake is able to use his material properties to help people; he breaks the lady's fall and allows her to bounce; he floats, he can stick over a hole. Explore household materials (cloth, polystyrene, newspaper, cling wrap, foam rubber) to see which of the situations they would be useful in, if any.

Domestic Science – (or is it called Food technology these days?) – Make pancakes. Follow some different recipes to make different types of pancake. Which do the children prefer?

Title: The Mean Monkey
Author: Rachel DelaHaye

Genre: Fiction
Word count: 264

Overview

Babbo has found a tree full of coconuts and he doesn't want to share them. Even Kamal's offer of help to pick the coconuts doesn't shift Babbo from his mean attitude. Kamal's cunning plan results in a much fairer approach to sharing the coconuts – but does Babbo realise that he has been tricked?

Learning outcomes

Children can:

- monitor their own errors and show a greater degree of independent self-correction
- reread to check meaning is conveyed through phrasing and expression
- discuss the story to demonstrate understanding.

Developing reading comprehension

- Children can explore Babbo's motives for his behaviour. Was he really being mean?
- Extensive use of dialogue allows children to explore how characters are feeling and reacting to the situation.

Grammar and sentence structure

- Speech punctuation indicates the different characters speaking, such as the conversation between Babbo and Kamal on page 5. Attending to punctuation is key to gaining the full meaning of the text and reading with appropriate expression.
- Sentence lengths vary to create effect, for example using short sentences in dialogue: *'Look at me'* on page 2, *'This is my tree'* on page 5.

Word meaning and spelling

- Multi syllabic words (*'himself'*, *'coconut'*) can be read by identifying parts of words.
- Opportunity to rehearse automatic, fast recognition of high-frequency words.

Curriculum links

Science and Nature – Monkeys are primarily leaf eaters, but most are omnivores. Children could use the internet and non-fiction texts to explore what monkeys and baboons eat.

Literacy – Babbo has behaved badly. The children could write a letter from Babbo to the monkeys, apologising for being mean and promising to share the coconuts in futures.

Mapping and Correlation Chart

Mapping and Correlation Chart (Book Bands PINK A to BLUE)

Band	Title	Fiction/ non-fiction	Author	Cambridge Assessment International Education Primary English Curriculum Framework Links	International Primary Curriculum links	IB Primary Years Program topic links	Cambridge Global English Unit links
PINK A	Arif Goes Shopping	F	Charlotte al-Qadi	Understand that one spoken word corresponds with one written word. Read aloud from simple books independently.	Early Years Shopping	How we organize ourselves	Grade 1 Unit 2 Family Time
PINK A	Jamila Finds a Friend	F	Alison Hawes	Know that in English, print is read from left to right and top to bottom. Understand that one spoken word corresponds with one written word.	Early years Family and Friends	Who we are	Grade 1 Unit 1 Welcome to School
PINK A	A Hot Day	F	Alison Hawes	Understand that one spoken word corresponds with one written word. Make simple inferences about characters and events to show understanding.	Early Years Animals	How the world works	Grade 1 Unit 8 Wonderful Water
PINK A	Packing my Bag	F	Alison Hawes	Read a range of common words on sight. Make links to own experiences.	Early Years All about me	Who we are	Grade 1 Unit 1 Welcome to School
PINK A	Please Stop, Sara!	F	Kathryn Harper	Use phonic knowledge to read decodable words. Anticipate what happens next in a story.	Early Years Family and Friends	Who we are	Grade 1 Unit 8 Wonderful Water
PINK A	Water	NF	Claire Llewellyn	Understand that one spoken word corresponds with one written word. Know that in English, print is read from left to right and top to bottom.	Early Years Sand and water	Sharing the planet	Grade 1 Unit 8 Wonderful Water
PINK A	The Sun is Up	NF	Claire Llewellyn	Understand that one spoken word corresponds with one written word. Read a range of common words on sight.	Milestone 1 Seeing the light	How the world works	Grade 1 Unit 8 Wonderful Water
PINK A	Games	NF	Lynne Rickards	Read aloud from simple books independently. Make links to own experiences.	Early Years All about Me	Who we are	Grade 1 Unit 3 Fun and games
PINK A	Animal Homes	NF	Lauri Kubuitsile	Understand that one spoken word corresponds with one written word. Know that in English, print is read from left to right and top to bottom.	Early years Houses and Homes; Animals	Where we are in place and time	Grade 1 Unit 5 On the farm
PINK A	Photos	F	Alison Hawes	Demonstrate an understanding that one spoken word corresponds with one written word; Know that in English, print is read from left to right and top to bottom.	Family and Friends	Who we are	Grade 1 Unit 2 Family Time

Band	Title	Fiction/ non-fiction	Author	Cambridge Assessment International Education Primary English Curriculum Framework Links	International Primary Curriculum links	IB Primary Years Program topic links	Cambridge Global English Unit links
PINK A	The Tractor	F	Alison Hawes	Anticipate what happens next in a story. Talk about events in a story and make simple inferences about characters and events to show understanding.	Family and Friends; Transport	How we express ourselves Who we are	Grade 1 Unit 5 On the farm
PINK A	I Can Help	NF	Lynne Rickards	Demonstrate an understanding that one spoken word corresponds with one written word; Know that in English, print is read from left to right and top to bottom.	All about me	Who we are	Grade 1 Unit 7 Let's go!
PINK B	My Dad is a Builder	F	Lynne Rickards	Make simple inferences about characters and events to show understanding. Know that in English, print is read from left to right and top to bottom.	Early years Houses and Homes	Where we are in place and time	Grade 1 Unit 4 Making things
PINK B	The Last Lemon	F	Alison Hawes	Read a range of common words on sight. Anticipate what happens next in a story.	Early years Animals	How we organize ourselves	Grade 1 Unit 4 Making things
PINK B	Leela can Skate	F	Alison Hawes	Use phonic knowledge to read decodable words. Anticipate what happens next in a story.	Early Years All About Me; Clothes;	Who we are	Grade 1 Unit 6 My five senses
PINK B	Omar's First Day at School	F	Shoua Fakhouri	Understand that one spoken word corresponds with one written word. Make links to own experiences.	Early Years All about me	How we organize ourselves	Grade 1 Unit 1 Welcome to School
PINK B	Our Den	F	Gabby Pritchard	Understand that one spoken word corresponds with one written word. Know that in English, print is read from left to right and top to bottom.	Early Years Family and Friends; Let's Pretend	Who we are	Grade 1 Unit 4 Making things
PINK B	Looking After Animals	NF	Claire Llewellyn	Read aloud from simple books independently. Make links to own experiences.	Early Years Animals	Sharing the planet	Grade 1 Unit 5 On the farm
PINK B	At the Market	NF	Alison Hawes	Know that in English, print is read from left to right and top to bottom.	Early years Shopping	How we organize ourselves	Grade 1 Unit 2 Family Time
PINK B	Who Lays Eggs?	NF	Claire Llewellyn	Know that in English, print is read from left to right and top to bottom. Use phonic knowledge to read decodable words.	Early years Animals	How the world works	Grade 1 Unit 5 On the farm
PINK B	Where do they Grow?	NF	Lynne Rickards	Read a range of common words on sight. Read aloud from simple books independently.	Early Years Food; Plants and flowers	How the world works	Grade 1 Unit 5 On the farm

Band	Title	Fiction/ non-fiction	Author	Cambridge Assessment International Education Primary English Curriculum Framework Links	International Primary Curriculum links	IB Primary Years Program topic links	Cambridge Global English Unit links
PINK B	Hello, Baby	F	Glen Franklin and Sue Bodman	Hear, read and write initial letter sounds. Know the name and most common sound associated with every letter in the English alphabet.	Family and Friends	Who we are	Grade 1 Unit 2 Family Time
PINK B	School Lunch	F	Glen Franklin and Sue Bodman	Hear, read and write initial letter sounds. Know the name and most common sound associated with every letter in the English alphabet.	Food	Who we are	Grade 1 Unit 1 Welcome to School
PINK B	Where are you Going?	F	Glen Franklin and Sue Bodman	Demonstrate an understanding that one spoken word corresponds with one written word.	Family and Friends	Who we are	Grade 1 Unit 3 Fun and games
RED	Bedtime on the Farm	F	Alex Eeles	Anticipate what happens next in a story. Make links to own experiences.	Early Years Animals	How the world works: How we organize ourselves	Grade 1 Unit 5 On the farm
RED	Leopard and his Spots	F	Kathryn Harper	Understand that one spoken word corresponds with one written word. Anticipate what happens next in a story.	Early Years Patterns	Who we are	Grade 1 Unit 4 Making things
RED	The Enormous Watermelon	F	Alison Hawes	Use phonic knowledge to read decodable words. Make links to own experiences.	Early years Shopping	How we organize ourselves	Grade 1 Unit 2 Family Time
RED	Omar can Help	F	Lynne Rickards	Read a range of common words on sight. Use phonic knowledge to read decodable words.	Early years Family and Friends	Who we are	Grade 1 Unit 1 Welcome to School
RED	Seagull	F	Kathryn Harper	Understand that one spoken word corresponds with one written word. Anticipate what happens next in a story.	Early Years Animals	Sharing the planet	Grade 1 Unit 8 Wonderful Water
RED	Look! It's Baby Duck	F	Gabby Pritchard	Read a range of common words on sight. Use phonic knowledge to read decodable words.	Early Years Changes	Who we are	Grade 1 Unit 5 On the farm
RED	Our Senses	NF	Claire Llewellyn	Read labels, lists and captions to find information. Know that in English, print is read from left to right and top to bottom.	Early Years All about me	Who we are	Grade 1 Unit 6 My five senses
RED	In the Sea	NF	Claire Llewellyn	Read labels, lists and captions to find information. Use phonic knowledge to read decodable words.	Early Years Animals	How the world works	Grade 1 Unit 8 Wonderful Water

Band	Title	Fiction/non-fiction	Author	Cambridge Assessment International Education Primary English Curriculum Framework Links	International Primary Curriculum links	IB Primary Years Program topic links	Cambridge Global English Unit links
RED	The Weather Today	NF	Claire Llewellyn	Understand that one spoken word corresponds with one written word. Aware that texts for different purposes look different.	Early Years Sand and Water	How the world works	Grade 1 Unit 8 Wonderful water
RED	Houses and Homes	NF	Lynne Rickards	Use phonic knowledge to read decodable words. Read labels, lists and captions to find information.	Early Years Houses and Homes	Where we are in place and time	Grade 1 Unit 3 Fun and games
RED	Imani's Library Book	F	Alison Hawes	Anticipate what happens next in a story. Read a range of common words on sight.	Who Am I?	How we express ourselves	Grade 1 Unit 2 Family Time
RED	What Little Kitten Wants	F	Kathryn Harper	Read a range of common words on sight. Use phonic knowledge to read decodable words.	I'm Alive	Who we are	Grade 1 Unit 2 Family time
YELLOW	A House for Snail	F	Vivian French	Use phonic knowledge to read decodable words. Make simple inferences about characters and events to show understanding.	Milepost 1 Habitats	Where we are in place and time	Grade 1 Unit 5 On the farm
YELLOW	Diego Fandango	F	Lynne Rickards	Know that in English, print is read from left to right and top to bottom. Make links to own experiences.	Milepost 1 Things people do; Let's Celebrate	How we express ourselves	Grade 1 Unit 6 My five senses
YELLOW	Late for School	F	Claire Llewellyn	Read a range of common words on sight. Make links to own experiences.	Milepost 1 From A to B	Where we are in place and time	Grade 1 Unit 1 Welcome to School; Grade 1 Unit 7 Let's go!
YELLOW	Oh Bella!	F	Lauri Kubuitsile	Read a range of common words on sight. Use phonic knowledge to read decodable words.	Milepost 1 A day in the life	Who we are	Grade 1 Unit 2 Family time; Grade 1 unit 5 On the farm
YELLOW	Little Tiger Hu can Roar!	F	Gabby Pritchard	Make simple inferences about characters and events to show understanding. Make links to own experiences.	Milepost 1 Science - Earth - Our home	Where we are in place and time	Grade 1 Unit 3 Fun and games
YELLOW	My School	NF	Shouha Fakhouri	Read aloud from simple books independently. Make links to own experiences.	Milepost 1 A Day in the Life	How we organize ourselves	Grade 1 Unit 1 Welcome to school
YELLOW	Playgrounds	NF	Lynne Rickards	Read aloud from simple books independently. Make links to own experiences.	Milepost 1 Science - what's it made of?; Buildings	Who we are	Grade 1 Unit 3 Fun and games
YELLOW	Stars	NF	Lauri Kubuitsile	Read labels, lists and captions to find information. Know the parts of a book, e.g. title page, contents.	Milepost 1 Seeing the Light	How the world works	Grade 2 Unit 7 Our green earth

Band	Title	Fiction/non-fiction	Author	Cambridge Assessment International Education Primary English Curriculum Framework Links	International Primary Curriculum links	IB Primary Years Program topic links	Cambridge Global English Unit links
YELLOW	Help!	F	Gabby Pritchard	Read a range of common words on sight. Use phonic knowledge to read decodable words.	The stories people tell	How we organise ourselves	Grade 2 Unit 6 Bugs: Fact and fiction
YELLOW	The Boy Who Said No	F	Alex Eeles	Make links to own experiences. Identify sentences in a text.	A day in the life, Who am I?	How we express ourselves	Grade 1 Unit 2 Family time
YELLOW	The Big City	NF	Lynne Rickards	Make links to own experiences. Read aloud independently from simple books.	Science- Earth- our home Our world- The Environment	Where we are in place and time	Grade 1 Unit 7 Let's go!
YELLOW	Where are my shoes?	F	Sue Bodman and Glen Franklin	Identify sentences in a text. Talk about events in a story and make simple inferences about characters and events to show understanding.	A day in the life: things people do All dressed up: clothes	Who we are	Grade 1 Unit 2 Family time
BLUE	Lost!	F	Gabby Pritchard	Anticipate what happens next in a story. Make links to own experiences.	Milepost 1 Flowers and Insects	Who we are; Where we are in place and time	Grade 2 Unit 6 Bugs: Fact and fiction
BLUE	Suli's Big Race	F	Alex Eeles	Make simple inferences about characters and events to show understanding. Make links to own experiences.	Milepost 1 The First Olympians; PE - MP1 - Specialist Unit	Who we are	Grade 1 Unit 3 Fun and games; Grade 2 Unit 3 Ready, steady, go!
BLUE	A Day at the Museum	F	Sibel Sagner, Sevi Senocak and Inci Kartal	Make simple inferences about characters and events to show understanding. Make links to own experiences.	Milepost 1 The Magic Toymaker	Where we are in place and time	Grade 1 Unit 4 Making things
BLUE	It's Much Too Early	F	Ian Whybrow	Anticipate what happens next in a story. Make links to own experiences.	Milepost 1 Let's Celebrate; The stories people tell	Who we are	Grade 2 Unit 5 Let's count and measure
BLUE	The Pumpkin Monster	F	Susan Gates	Anticipate what happens next in a story. Make links to own experiences.	Milepost 1 Science – Greenfingers; The stories people tell	Sharing the planet	Grade 1 Unit 5 On the farm
BLUE	My First Train Trip	NF	Lynne Rickards	Use phonic knowledge to read decodable words. Make links to own experiences.	Milepost 1 From A to B; Hooray…Let's go on Holiday!	Where we are in place and time	Grade 1 Unit 7 Let's go!
BLUE	Making a Car	NF	Claire Llewellyn	Read labels, lists and captions to find information. Aware that texts for different purposes look different.	Milepost 1 Things people do; What's it made of; From A to B	How we organize ourselves	Grade 1 Unit 4 Making things
BLUE	All Kinds of Plants	NF	Anita Ganeri	Read labels, lists and captions to find information. Read a range of common words on sight.	Milepost 1 Science- Greenfingers; Flowers and Insects	How the world works	Grade 2 Unit 7 Our green earth

Band	Title	Fiction/ non-fiction	Author	Cambridge Assessment International Education Primary English Curriculum Framework Links	International Primary Curriculum links	IB Primary Years Program topic links	Cambridge Global English Unit links
BLUE	On the Track	NF	Claire Llewellyn	Read labels, lists and captions to find information. Aware that texts for different purposes look different.	Milepost 1 The First Olympians	How the world works?	Grade 2 Unit 3 Ready, steady, go!; Grade 1 Unit 3 Fun and games
BLUE	Crabs	NF	Ralph Hall	Identify sentences in a text. Read labels, lists and captions to find information.	Science- Live and Let Live: living things	How the world works	Grade 1 Unit 8 Wonderful water
BLUE	The Show and Tell Day	F	Sibel Sagner	Talk about events in a story and make simple inferences about characters and events to show understanding. Make links to own experiences.	Who am I?	How we express ourselves	Grade 1 Unit 1 Welcome to School
BLUE	The Big Pancake	F	Susan Gates	Make links to own experiences. Identify sentences in a text.	We are what we eat- food; A day in the life- things people do	Who we are	Grade 1 Unit 7 Let's go!
BLUE	The Mean Monkey	F	Rachel DelaHaye	Identify sentences in a text; Anticipate what happens next in a story.	Who am I?	Who we are Sharing the planet	Grade 1 Unit 3 Fun and games

Reading Assessment

Successful guided reading relies on the texts being at just the right instructional level: the child needs to read the book with a degree of independence but with some challenges and opportunity for new learning to be taught in the guided reading lesson. If the book is too easy, no new learning can occur. If it is too difficult, then comprehension breaks down completely. *Cambridge Reading Adventures* includes a Benchmark text at each band. To ascertain that a child is ready to progress to the next band, teachers carry out the benchmark assessment, beginning with an individual running record of continuous text reading.

Taking a running record

Give the child a copy of the book. The text will have been unseen before this point. Follow the instructions on the record sheet, providing an overview of the book and locating the place to start the reading.

As the child reads, record the reading behaviour using the following procedures:

Tick each word read correctly	✓ ✓ ✓ ✓ ✓ 'The baby duck can walk,' ✓ ✓ ✓ said Grey Mouse.
Record incorrect responses above the word and record as an error.	✓ ✓ ✓ ✓ run 'The baby duck can walk,' ✓ ✓ ✓ said Grey Mouse.
Record any successful self-corrections by writing **SC** next to the original error. Record as a self-correction.	✓ ✓ ✓ ✓ run ǀ SC 'The baby duck can walk,' ✓ ✓ ✓ said Grey Mouse.
Use a dash when a child omits a word or gives no response. This is counted as an error.	✓ – ✓ ✓ ✓ 'The baby duck can walk,' ✓ ✓ ✓ said Grey Mouse.
If a child inserts a word, write it into the running record. This is counted as an error.	✓ little ✓ ✓ ✓ 'The baby duck can walk,' ✓ ✓ ✓ said Grey Mouse.
Record **T** if you decide to tell the child the correct word. This is counted as an error.	✓ ✓ ✓ ✓ run ǀ 'The baby duck can walk,' ǀ T ✓ ✓ – ǀ said Grey Mouse. ǀ T
Record **A** if the child appeals to you for help if unsure of a word or after an incorrect response. Encourage them to try. Record **SC** if the child is able to read the word, or tell them the word, recording **T** and counting this as an error	✓ ✓ ✓ ✓ – ǀ A ǀ 'The baby duck can walk,' ǀ T ✓ ✓ mum ǀ A ǀ SC said Grey Mouse. ǀ
Record **R** above the word if the child repeats it. Indicate the number of times the word is reread. Repetition is **not** counted as an error.	✓ ✓R ✓ ✓ ✓ 'The baby duck can walk,' ✓R^2 ✓ ✓ said Grey Mouse.

Record **R** with an arrow if the child reads back in the sentence and repeats more than one word. Rereading is **not** counted as an error.	✓ ✓ ✓ R ✓ ✓ 'The baby duck can walk,' ✓ ✓ ✓ said Grey Mouse.
If the child becomes confused, stop the reading and say 'Try that again'. Bracket the confused passage and write **TTA**. This is counted as an error.	[✓ ✓ — is running] TTA 'The baby duck can walk,' ✓ ✓ ✓ said Grey Mouse.

Scoring a running record

The aim of this benchmarking assessment is to ascertain whether the child is ready to move to the next band. To do so, a child would need to be reading at around 94% accuracy at the current band.

Finding an accuracy rate

Look at your running record of the child's reading behaviours. Total how many errors you recorded in the errors column (see page 83 for a completed example).

Divide the total number of words by the number of errors in the running record to find the error ratio:

> 64 (words in the running record)
> divided by 6 (number of errors)
> = a ratio of **1:10**

Next, convert the ratio to an accuracy rate, using the table below:

Error ratio	Accuracy rate	
1:100	99%	
1:50	98%	Easy: At 95% and above, indicates that texts are easy for the child to read at this band.
1:35	97%	
1:25	96%	
1:20	95%	
1:17	94%	Instructional: At between 90% - 94%, texts are read more accurately, with fluency and understanding, whilst an element of challenge remains.
1:14	93%	
1:12.5	92%	
1:11.75	91%	
1:10	90%	Hard: Below 90%, the reading becomes too difficult: the child is unable to problem-solve effectively and comprehension breaks down
1:9	89%	
1:8	87.5%	
1:7	85.5%	
1:6	83%	
1:5	80%	

> An error ratio of 1: 10
> converts to an accuracy rate of 90%

Record the accuracy rate on the running record form, indicating if this text is at an easy, instructional or hard level for this child.

Finding the self-correction rate

Total the number of self-corrections recorded in the second column (page 83 provides an example). Remember, self-corrections are not errors; they indicate reading behaviours the child has initiated independently.

To calculate the self-correction rate, add together the total number of errors and the total number of self-corrections. Then, divide this figure by the number of self-corrections only:

> 9 (Total number of errors and self-corrections)
> divided by 3 (number of self-corrections)
> = a self-correction ratio of **1:3**

Record this information on the running record form.

Reading Assessment

Analysing the child's reading behaviours

An accuracy rate will give a comparable measure of progress, but it does not provide information about the reading behaviours the child is using and how effective these are. These reading behaviours, or strategies, are indicators of how the child is using what he knows to process text. By analysing the reading behaviours captured on the running record, teachers can look more closely at what sources of information the child is using or neglecting.

Clay[10] identified three sources of information readers attend to when reading:

The meaning – the information gained from knowledge about the subject or story, or from the supportive illustrations - does what has been read make sense?

A child reading:

‾‾✓‾‾✓‾‾bird‾‾✓‾‾✓‾‾
'The baby duck can walk'

is likely to have been led by meaning.

The syntax – the support offered by grammatical language structures and punctuation: does what has been read sound right?

A child reading:

‾‾✓‾‾✓‾‾✓‾‾is‾‾✓‾‾
'The baby duck can walk'

may well be using the grammatical sentence structure up to that point in the sentence.

The visual information – the letters and words in print on the page - does what has been read look right?

A child reading:

‾‾✓‾‾✓‾‾dog‾‾✓‾‾✓‾‾
'The baby duck can walk'

has noticed the first letter 'd' so has used a source of print information at error.

---

[10] Clay, M. M. (2013). *An Observation Survey of Early Literacy Achievement*. 3rd Edition. Auckland, N.Z.: Heinemann

When these three sources of information are in balance, reading is accurate. Children's reading errors reveal if they are relying on one source predominantly, or if they are neglecting to use one source effectively. This will change over time.

Of course, sometimes children may use more than one cue source at a time. As teachers, we can never know exactly what caused a child to make an error. We can only observe the behaviour and consider the most effective way to help that child solve the problem.

Analysing self-correction

Self-corrections are not errors; however, in order to fully understand what led the child to self-correct, we first have to analyse the error that led to that self-correction. Again, this cannot be certain – we can only make an assumption based on what we know of the child's previous reading response and the challenges in this particular text.

A child reading:

‾‾✓‾‾✓‾‾dog | SC ✓ ✓
The baby duck | can walk

is likely to have used the initial letter as a source of visual information but self-corrected based on the meaning of the text, knowing the story is about a duck, cross-referencing to the pictures of the duck to support that meaning.

A child reading:

‾‾✓‾‾✓‾‾✓‾‾is | SC ✓
The baby duck can | walk

is probably using visual information to self-correct a syntactic error that sounded right at the point of error but didn't look right.

Completing the running record analysis

First, look at all the errors, including those that were then self-corrected. Consider what sources of information the child was using at the point the error occurred.

Decide if the error was lead predominantly by meaning **(M)**, or by the sentence structure and grammar **(S)** or by the visual information **(V)**, or a combination of any of these. For example, an error can often call upon meaning and syntax, such as the child reading 'run' for 'walk'. Record the errors at each source of information in the first set of grey columns **'Error Analysis'**. Please note that omissions and insertions, whilst still counting as errors, are not analysed.

Now look back at initial errors that were then self-corrected. Follow the same procedure, recording as M, S and/or V to consider what sources of information the child used that led to formulating a correct response. Record each source of information used to self-correct in the second set of grey columns **'S/C Analysis'**.

There is a worked example of a running record analysis on page 83.

Comprehension assessment

Cambridge Reading Adventures benchmark assessments also provide teachers with opportunity to consider progression in comprehension. Comprehension skills are developmental and the complexity aligns with that of a child's literacy development.

Benchmark texts are designed to support teachers assess that development. Question prompts are provided to help assess understanding.

The comprehension assessment takes place **after** the text has been read and the running record taken. Begin by asking the child to retell the story in his own words. This will have been an unseen text. Retelling will help the teacher assess how well the child is able to demonstrate understanding.

Questions to assess understanding

Recalling: At the Early stage, comprehension questions are predominantly **recalling questions**, like those designed to assess *'What can Baby Duck do?'*; the answers are literal and can be specifically drawn from the text. Answers need to be accurate although sometimes there will be multiple choices.

Inferring: As children progress through the bands, the balance shifts to a greater proportion of **inferring questions**, such as *'Why do you think Brown Mouse and Grey Mouse shouted 'Help!''* which require children to read 'between the lines' of the specific information in the text in order to draw conclusions and to gain meaning. There will often be more than one plausible response.

Responding: Children develop their comprehension skills further in the Transitional stage. There will be fewer recalling questions. Now children are asked to 'go beyond the text' to explain, evaluate and comment on the content, and to demonstrate links with other texts they have read. There will often be multiple, plausible and reasonable responses to these **responding questions** such as *'Did you like this story? Can you tell me why/why not?'* Teachers will make a judgement based on the quality of the explanation and their knowledge of the child.

The chart below demonstrates how the balance of types of question develops from Early to Transitional bands.

Band	Recalling	Inferring	Responding
Pink A	3	1	
Pink B	3	1	
Red	3	1	
Yellow	3	2	1
Blue	3	2	1
Green	3	2	1
Orange	3	3	1
Turquoise	3	3	1
Purple	2	3	2
Gold	2	3	2
White	2	3	2

Progression of questions in *Cambridge Reading Adventures* Benchmark Texts

Score the number of questions answered correctly on the assessment summary.

Completing the Benchmark Assessment Summary

The Benchmark Assessment Summary is designed to pull together all the information gathered from the running record analysis, comprehension questions and from the teacher's own observations during the assessment. Based on this information, teachers will decide whether a child is ready to progress to the next band, or make recommendations to target particular aspects of language or reading behaviours whilst remaining at the current band. Page 84 provides a worked example.

Summary of observations during the assessment

Reading Strategies:

Record the error and self-correction rates on the summary form.

Looking at your analysis of errors and self corrections, consider:

- Did you notice a particular pattern of responses? For example, did the child overlook letter and word information in their errors?

- Are there any successful self-corrections? What were the sources of information that resulted in successful self-correction? Did the child look more carefully at the print information, perhaps? Or did they realise that it didn't make sense?

- Did the child try to make their reading make sense? Did they attempt to sound out or use parts of words to work things out?

- If the child is ready to begin working at the next band, you will see evidence of the child trying to work things out and in the majority of cases, making errors that make sense.

Using Print:

Particularly at the Early stage, print concepts are being established. It is important to note:

- How well did the child control left-to-right directionality and the return sweep on texts with multiple lines?

- Was one-to-one matching secure?

- Did the child read along the words, slowly checking and sounding out words which are phonically regular?

- Did the child notice and use chunks in words of more than one syllable?

- Were print features (such as commas, speech punctuation, layout) noticed and used?

A child that is regularly making errors with using print is not yet ready to read more challenging material and needs further work at the current band.

Fluency:

There is a clear link between fluency and comprehension. Children who read slowly and in a disjointed way often don't understand what they are reading. Things to note on your record are:

- Was the child reading in a phrased, fluent manner or was the reading disjointed and staccato-sounding?

- Was finger-pointing slowing the reading down?

- Did the child attend to punctuation to support reading for meaning?

- Was intonation appropriate?

- Were clues in print (such as words in bold or italic for emphasis) used for expression?

Summary of Reading Comprehension skills:

Retelling task:

- Could the child retell the text independently? Did the child embellish and add further information?

- To what extent did he rely on the pictures in the text to support the retelling? Were the pictures interpreted correctly?

- Did you have to prompt or assist in order to complete the retelling?

- Was the retelling confident and succinct?

Sequencing ideas:

- How well was the retelling structured?

- Were events followed in sequence?

- Were all the main events included?

- Was notice taken of additional events, subsidiary to the main events?

Control of vocabulary

- Was the vocabulary appropriate?
- Did it relate to the book?
- Did the child seek to explain or expand upon subject-specific vocabulary?
- Did it match the tone, style or genre of the text read?

Comprehension

Add the comprehension outcomes for recalling, inferring and responding, as appropriate.

Note down any particular information about how the child approached the comprehension questions, for example:

- Did he carefully reference back to the text to support his answers?
- Does he have difficulty in moving beyond the more literal questions?

- Was he misled by illustrations when information needed to answer the question was not pictured explicitly?

Think about what might have led the child to an incorrect response, and consider the plausibility of the answer.

Recommendations

This section enables the teacher to review the observations and consider the next steps for this child. The teacher will then need to look at the text characteristics for the next band, (see page 28 in this Teaching and Assessment Guide), and decide, on the basis of the evidence collected, whether the child is ready to progress.

NB: This judgement is not made on the accuracy rate alone, but by looking across all the elements of reading and comprehension assessed at each benchmark point.

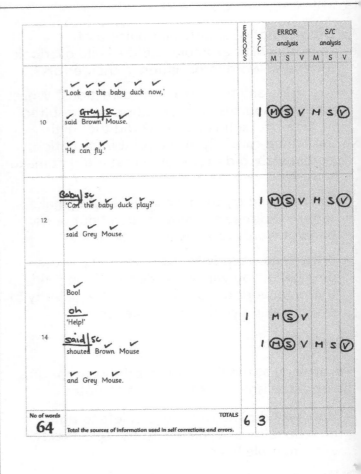

RED BAND Benchmark Assessment

NAME: Aisha

Benchmark Assessment Summary

CLASS GROUP: Tigers

Look! It's Baby Duck

DATE: 5th Feb. 2015

Accuracy:

☐ **HARD**
Errors: more than 1:10

☑ **INSTRUCTIONAL**
Errors: between 1:10 and 1:25

☐ **EASY**
Errors; fewer than 1:25

Summary of Observations during the assessment

Reading Strategies: Errors predominantly meaning-led with SC using print information. Syntax mostly maintained. Grammatical errors indicate she is using sentence structure to predict.

Using Print: Aisha mostly controls 1-1 matching, with some mismatches when meaning overrides print information. Finger pointing used occasionally.

Fluency: The story sounded good and was phrased appropriately.

Summary of Reading Comprehension Skills

Retelling task: Some confusion about what each of the mice said. Ending was omitted and the focus was mainly on Baby Duck's actions.

Sequencing ideas: Difficulty in identifying Brown Mouse and Grey Mouse + their roles in the story. The build-up of events was not clear.

Control of vocabulary: Vocab used was appropriate to the text. Sometimes used 'Baby' rather than 'Baby Duck'.

Comprehension:

Recalling: ①/3   Inferring: ⓪/1   Total Score: ①

Comments: Aisha did not seem to understand why the Baby Duck shouted, or why the mice were scared.

Recommendations: Aisha now needs to attend more closely to print to support her developing use of meaning + structure. In guided reading lessons, I will need to draw her attention to visual mismatches, prompting her to check that what she says matches what she can see on the page. Texts at Red band will provide greater support, and further guided reading at this band will be beneficial.

Move to Yellow Band? Y Ⓝ

95

Book Bands Class Progress Tracker / Early Reading

Child's name	Pink A	Pink B	Red	Yellow	Blue

PINK A BAND Benchmark Assessment

Error ratio:

Accuracy rate:

Self correction ratio:

Orientation for assessment:

'Sara finds lots of things to play with. What a noise she makes. Let's see who will make her stop.'

PAGE	TITLE: **Please, Stop Sara!** BAND: Pink A	ERRORS	S/C	ERROR analysis			S/C analysis		
				M	S	V	M	S	V
2	Sara finds the drum.								
3	Please stop Sara!								
4	Sara finds the pot.								
5	Please stop, Sara!								
6	Sara finds the car.								
7	Please stop, Sara!								
8	Sara finds the duck.								

		E R R O R S	S / C	ERROR analysis			S/C analysis		
				M	S	V	M	S	V
9	Please stop, Sara!								
10	Sara finds the radio.								
11	Please stop, Sara!								
12	Sara finds the television.								
13	Please stop, Sara!								
14	Sara finds the book.								
15	Don't stop, Adam!								
No of words **49**	TOTALS Total the sources of information used in self corrections and errors.								

PINK A BAND Benchmark Assessment

NAME:

Comprehension assessment

CLASS GROUP:

Please Stop, Sara!

DATE:

Retelling task: *(Tick and comment as appropriate)*

Retold independently. ⬭

Retold using the pictures to support ⬭

Retold with some adult support ⬭

Sequencing Ideas: *(Tick and comment as appropriate)*

Followed the correct sequence of events ⬭

Mentioned some of the events in sequence ⬭

Events retold out of sequence ⬭

Control of Vocabulary: *(Tick and comment as appropriate)*

Used vocabulary of the book and their own vocabulary appropriately and interchangeably ⬭

Used the vocabulary of the book appropriately ⬭

Unfocused or inaccurate use of vocabulary denoting lack of understanding ⬭

Questioning to assess understanding   *(Tick as appropriate)*

Recalling:

'Look at this page' (pages 2/3) 'Who is playing the drum?   ⬭
(Sara)

What happens when Sara finds the duck?   ⬭
(She splashes in the bath; She makes a mess on the floor; She gets water on the floor; She makes the cat wet.)

What happened when Sara finds the book?   ⬭
(Adam reads it to Sara; Sara sits down; Sara is quiet; Sara listens to Adam reading.)

Score: ⬭

Inferring:

Why do you think Mum and Dad want Sara to stop finding things to play with?   ⬭
(They don't like the noise; Sara is too noisy; They want her to be quiet.)

Score: ⬭

Total Score: ⬭

!K A BAND Benchmark Assessment

NAME:

Benchmark Assessment Summary

CLASS GROUP:

Please Stop, Sara!

DATE:

Accuracy:

◯ **HARD**
Errors: more than 1:10

◯ **INSTRUCTIONAL**
Errors: between 1:10 and 1:25

◯ **EASY**
Errors; fewer than 1:25

Summary of Observations during the assessment

Reading Strategies:

Using Print:

Fluency:

Summary of Reading Comprehension Skills

Retelling task:

Sequencing ideas:

Control of vocabulary:

Comprehension:

Recalling: ◯ / 3   **Inferring:** ◯ / 1   **Total Score:** ◯

Comments:

Recommendations:

Move to Pink B Band? Y/N

PINK B BAND Benchmark Assessment

Error ratio:

Accuracy rate:

Self correction ratio:

Orientation for assessment:

'Sami and Max want to build a den. Sami got some things for the den.
Let's see what their den looked like when they finished.'

PAGE	TITLE: **Our Den** BAND: Pink B	ERRORS	S/C	ERROR analysis			S/C analysis		
				M	S	V	M	S	V
2	'Look! I've got some blankets for the den,' said Sami. 'Good,' said Max.								
4	'Look! I've got some string for the den,' said Sami. 'Good,' said Max.								
6	'Look! I've got some pegs for the den,' said Sami. 'Good,' said Max.								

		ERRORS	S/C	ERROR analysis			S/C analysis		
				M	S	V	M	S	V
8	'Look! I've got a table for the den,' said Sami. 'Good,' said Max.								
10	'Look! I've got some chairs for the den,' said Sami. 'Good,' said Max.								
12	'Look! I've got some food for the den,' said Sami. 'Good,' said Max.								
14	'I've got a den,' said Max. 'Good,' said Sami.								
No of words **87**	**TOTALS** Total the sources of information used in self corrections and errors.								

PINK B BAND Benchmark Assessment

Comprehension assessment

Our Den

NAME:

CLASS GROUP:

DATE:

Retelling task: (Tick and comment as appropriate)

Retold independently.

Retold using the pictures to support

Retold with some adult support

○
○
○

Sequencing Ideas: (Tick and comment as appropriate)

Followed the correct sequence of events

Mentioned some of the events in sequence

Events retold out of sequence

○
○
○

Control of Vocabulary: (Tick and comment as appropriate)

Used vocabulary of the book and their own vocabulary appropriately and interchangeably

Used the vocabulary of the book appropriately

Unfocused or inaccurate use of vocabulary denoting lack of understanding

○
○
○

Questioning to assess understanding   (Tick as appropriate)

Recalling:

What do Sami and Max want to make?

(a den)   ○

Look at this page (pages 6/7). What did they use the string to do?   ○

(Hang the blanket on; To ties between two trees; To make the blanket stay up; To make the blanket into a tent.

If the child responds 'to make a den', prompt for a more precise answer: Yes, but what did they do with the string?)

Who brings the things for the den?

(Sami)   ○

Score: ○

Inferring:

What do you think they will do now the den is finished?   ○

(go inside; eat the food; sit on the chairs; play inside the den)

Score: ○

Total Score: ○

PINK B BAND Benchmark Assessment

Benchmark Assessment Summary

Our Den

NAME:

CLASS GROUP:

DATE:

Accuracy:

◯ **HARD**
Errors: more than 1:10

◯ **INSTRUCTIONAL**
Errors: between 1:10 and 1:25

◯ **EASY**
Errors; fewer than 1:25

Summary of Observations during the assessment

Reading Strategies:

Using Print:

Fluency:

Summary of Reading Comprehension Skills

Retelling task:

Sequencing ideas:

Control of vocabulary:

Comprehension:

Recalling: ◯ / 3   **Inferring:** ◯ / 1   **Total Score:** ◯

Comments:

Recommendations:

Move to Red Band? Y/N

RED BAND Benchmark Assessment

Error ratio:

Accuracy rate:

Self correction ratio:

Orientation for assessment:

"Brown Mouse and Grey Mouse saw Baby Duck in the nest. They watched him. But they hadn't realised just how clever Baby Duck is!"

PAGE	TITLE: Look! It's Baby Duck! BAND: Red	ERRORS	S/C	ERROR analysis			S/C analysis		
				M	S	V	M	S	V
2	'Look it's a Baby Duck,' said Brown Mouse.								
4	'The baby duck can walk,' said Grey Mouse.								
6	'The baby duck can quack, too,' said Brown Mouse.								
8	'Look at the baby duck,' said Grey Mouse. 'He can swim.'								

		E R R O R S	S / C	ERROR analysis			S/C analysis		
				M	S	V	M	S	V
10	'Look at the baby duck now,' said Brown Mouse. 'He can fly.'								
12	'Can the baby duck play?' said Grey Mouse.								
14	Boo! 'Help!' shouted Brown Mouse and Grey Mouse.								
No of words **64**	**TOTALS** **Total the sources of information used in self corrections and errors.**								

RED BAND Benchmark Assessment

Comprehension assessment

Look! It's Baby Duck

NAME:

CLASS GROUP:

DATE:

Retelling task: *(Tick and comment as appropriate)*

Retold independently. ◯

Retold using the pictures to support ◯

Retold with some adult support ◯

Sequencing Ideas: *(Tick and comment as appropriate)*

Followed the correct sequence of events ◯

Mentioned some of the events in sequence ◯

Events retold out of sequence ◯

Control of Vocabulary: *(Tick and comment as appropriate)*

Used vocabulary of the book and their own vocabulary appropriately and interchangeably ◯

Used the vocabulary of the book appropriately ◯

Unfocused or inaccurate use of vocabulary denoting lack of understanding ◯

Questioning to assess understanding *(Tick as appropriate)*

Recalling:

Look at this page' (pages 2/3) 'Who said 'Look it's a baby duck'? ◯
(Brown Mouse)

What can Baby Duck do? ◯
(walk, quack, swim, fly, play, shout Boo- a minimum of 3 needed to score as correct,
Prompt if needed by saying 'anything else?')

What happened when Brown Mouse and Grey Mouse tried to play with Baby Duck? ◯
(he shouted 'Boo!', he made them jump, he jumped out at them)

Score: ◯

Inferring:

Why do you think Brown Mouse and Grey Mouse shouted 'Help'? ◯
(Baby Duck made them jump, they were frightened, they didn't know he was behind them)

Score: ◯

Total Score: ◯

RED BAND Benchmark Assessment

Benchmark Assessment Summary

Look! It's Baby Duck

NAME:

CLASS GROUP:

DATE:

Accuracy:

◯ **HARD**
Errors: more than 1:10

◯ **INSTRUCTIONAL**
Errors: between 1:10 and 1:25

◯ **EASY**
Errors; fewer than 1:25

Summary of Observations during the assessment

Reading Strategies:

Using Print:

Fluency:

Summary of Reading Comprehension Skills

Retelling task:

Sequencing ideas:

Control of vocabulary:

Comprehension:

Recalling: ◯ / 3   **Inferring:** ◯ / 1   **Total Score:** ◯

Comments:

Recommendations:

Move to Yellow Band? Y/N

YELLOW BAND Benchmark Assessment

Error ratio:

Accuracy rate:

Self correction ratio:

Orientation for assessment:

"In this story, Little Tiger Hu likes playing games. He makes other animals in the jungle jump. How do you think he does that? Let's find out.'

PAGE	TITLE: **Little Tiger Hu Finds His Roar** BAND: Yellow	ERRORS	S/C	ERROR analysis			S/C analysis		
				M	S	V	M	S	V
2	Little Tiger Hu was very happy. 'I can ROAR,' he said. It was a BIG and SCARY roar! 'I can play a game,' he said.								
3	Tiger Hu saw Elephant. Slowly, slowly he went through the long grass. 'One, two, three, four ...'								
4	Roarrr! 'HELP!' shouted Elephant and he ran into the forest.								
5	Little Tiger Hu saw Hippo. Slowly, slowly he went round the big rocks. 'One, two, three, four ...'								
6	Roarrr! 'HELP!' shouted Hippo and he jumped into the river.								

		E R R O R S	S / C	ERROR analysis			S/C analysis		
				M	S	V	M	S	V
7	Little Tiger Hu saw Monkey. Slowly, slowly he climbed up a tree. 'One, two three, four …'								
8	Roarrr! 'HELP!' shouted Monkey and he ran up a big tree.								
9	Little Tiger Hu saw Hare. Slowly, slowly he went over a bridge … … into a green field. 'One, two, three, four …'								
11	Roarrr! 'Hello, Little Tiger Hu,' said Hare.								
12	'Why aren't you scared?' said Little Tiger Hu. 'You are silly,' said Hare. 'Babies are not scary, even if they have a big roar.'								
13	'We can play a new game,' said Little Tiger Hu. Little Tiger Hu and Hare went to play in the forest.								
No of words **177**	**TOTALS** Total the sources of information used in self corrections and errors.								

118

YELLOW BAND Benchmark Assessment

Comprehension assessment

Little Tiger Hu Can Roar

NAME:

CLASS GROUP:

DATE:

Retelling task: (Tick and comment as appropriate)

Retold independently. ☐

Retold using the pictures to support ☐

Retold with some adult support ☐

Sequencing Ideas: (Tick and comment as appropriate)

Followed the correct sequence of events ☐

Mentioned some of the events in sequence ☐

Events retold out of sequence ☐

Control of Vocabulary: (Tick and comment as appropriate)

Used vocabulary of the book and their own vocabulary appropriately and interchangeably ☐

Used the vocabulary of the book appropriately ☐

Unfocused or inaccurate use of vocabulary denoting lack of understanding ☐

Questioning to assess understanding

(Tick as appropriate)

Recalling:

What did Little Tiger Hu learn how to do? ☐

(roar)

Who did he scare? ☐

(Elephant, Hippo and Monkey)

What did Tiger Hu do with Hare? ☐

(tried to scare him, went to play with him)

Score: ☐

Inferring:

Why do you think that Tiger Hu went slowly, slowly, when he saw the animals? ☐

(So that they wouldn't know he was coming; So he could startle them; So they would jump when he roared.)

Why wasn't Hare scared? ☐

(He saw (or heard) Tiger Hu coming; He knew that Tiger Hu was only a baby.)

Score: ☐

Responding:

Hare and Tiger Hu go off to play a new game. Do you think they will be good friends? ☐

(Yes: Hare is not scared; Hare knows he is just a baby; Hare likes to play.

No: Tiger Hu will try and roar at him again; Tigers and hares do not play together;

Tiger Hu likes scaring people; He will do it again.)

Score: ☐

Total Score: ☐

YELLOW BAND Benchmark Assessment

Benchmark Assessment Summary

Little Tiger Hu Can Roar

NAME:

CLASS GROUP:

DATE:

Accuracy:

◯ **HARD**
Errors: more than 1:10

◯ **INSTRUCTIONAL**
Errors: between 1:10 and 1:25

◯ **EASY**
Errors; fewer than 1:25

Summary of Observations during the assessment

Reading Strategies:

Using Print:

Fluency:

Summary of Reading Comprehension Skills

Retelling task:

Sequencing ideas:

Control of vocabulary:

Comprehension:

Recalling: ◯ / 3   **Inferring:** ◯ / 2   **Responding:** ◯ / 1   **Total Score:** ◯ / 6

Comments:

Recommendations:

Move to Blue Band? Y/N

BLUE BAND Benchmark Assessment

Error ratio:

Accuracy rate:

Self correction ratio:

Orientation for assessment:
"In this story, Hanna's pumpkin grew into a monster and the villagers were really scared. They wanted Hanna to help them. I wonder if she is brave enough. Let's see."

PAGE	TITLE: The Pumpkin Monster BAND: Blue	ERRORS	S/C	ERROR analysis			S/C analysis		
				M	S	V	M	S	V
2	Hanna grew a big pumpkin. She was very happy with it.								
3	Everyone in the town came to see it. 'That's the biggest pumpkin we have ever seen!' they said.								
4	Hanna's pumpkin grew bigger and bigger until it was a monster!								
5	Now everyone was scared. 'Get rid of that pumpkin,' they said to Hanna.								
6	'I want food!' Shouted the Pumpkin Monster.								
7	And it rolled away, looking for things to eat.								
8	Hanna ran after the Pumpkin Monster.								
9	It rolled into a field of corn and gobbled it all up.								

		E R R O R S	S / C	ERROR analysis			S/C analysis		
				M	S	V	M	S	V
10	Soon the Pumpkin Monster was as big as a house. 'Stop eating our corn,' said Hanna, 'or we will be hungry!'								
11	But the monster did not stop eating. 'I want food!' it shouted and rolled on and on.								
12	Hanna chased the Pumpkin Monster into a forest. It rolled over some trees with sharp thorns.								
13	'PSST!' went the monster. 'Pssssssssst.' The Pumpkin Monster got smaller and smaller.								
14	Soon, the Pumpkin Monster was like a little orange puddle.								
15	'The Pumpkin Monster has gone,' said Hanna. 'Now we will not be hungry!' 'Hurray for Hanna!' said everyone.								
No of words **181**	**TOTALS** **Total the sources of information used in self corrections and errors.**								

BLUE BAND Benchmark Assessment

Comprehension assessment

The Pumpkin Monster

NAME:

CLASS GROUP:

DATE:

Retelling task: *(Tick and comment as appropriate)*

Retold independently. ◯

Retold using the pictures to support ◯

Retold with some adult support ◯

Sequencing Ideas: *(Tick and comment as appropriate)*

Followed the correct sequence of events ◯

Mentioned some of the events in sequence ◯

Events retold out of sequence ◯

Control of Vocabulary: *(Tick and comment as appropriate)*

Used vocabulary of the book and their own vocabulary appropriately and interchangeably ◯

Used the vocabulary of the book appropriately ◯

Unfocused or inaccurate use of vocabulary denoting lack of understanding ◯

Questioning to assess understanding

(Tick as appropriate)

Recalling:

What did people say about Hanna's pumpkin? ◯

(It was the biggest they'd ever seen; It was very big.)

What did the Pumpkin Monster want? ◯

(food/something to eat)

Where did the Pumpkin Monster roll? ◯

(a field of corn and a forest; both parts required)

Score: ◯

Inferring:

Why do you think the people were scared of the Pumpkin Monster? ◯

(It was very big; It was looking for food; They thought it would eat them/roll over them.)

What happened to the Pumpkin Monster? ◯

(It rolled over some sharp thorns; It popped/was deflated/burst/got smaller and smaller. Both elements required.

If only one part is given, prompt for more by repeating the part given and saying 'and....something else happened didn't it.

What else happened to the Pumpkin Monster?')

Score: ◯

Responding:

Do you think Hanna will grow more pumpkins? Why? ◯

Yes: Hanna is brave; Hanna knows what to do to defeat the Pumpkin Monster.

No: Hanna will be worried that a Pumpkin Monster will grow again; Hanna will be scared of pumpkins now.

Score: ◯

Total Score: ◯

BLUE BAND Benchmark Assessment

NAME:

Benchmark Assessment Summary

CLASS GROUP:

The Pumpkin Monster

DATE:

Accuracy:

◯ **HARD**
Errors: more than 1:10

◯ **INSTRUCTIONAL**
Errors: between 1:10 and 1:25

◯ **EASY**
Errors; fewer than 1:25

Summary of Observations during the assessment

Reading Strategies:

Using Print:

Fluency:

Summary of Reading Comprehension Skills

Retelling task:

Sequencing ideas:

Control of vocabulary:

Comprehension:

Recalling: ◯ / 3   **Inferring:** ◯ / 2   **Responding:** ◯ / 1   **Total Score:** ◯ / 6

Comments:

Recommendations:

Move to Green Band? Y/N